徐海鷹

三百山

前言

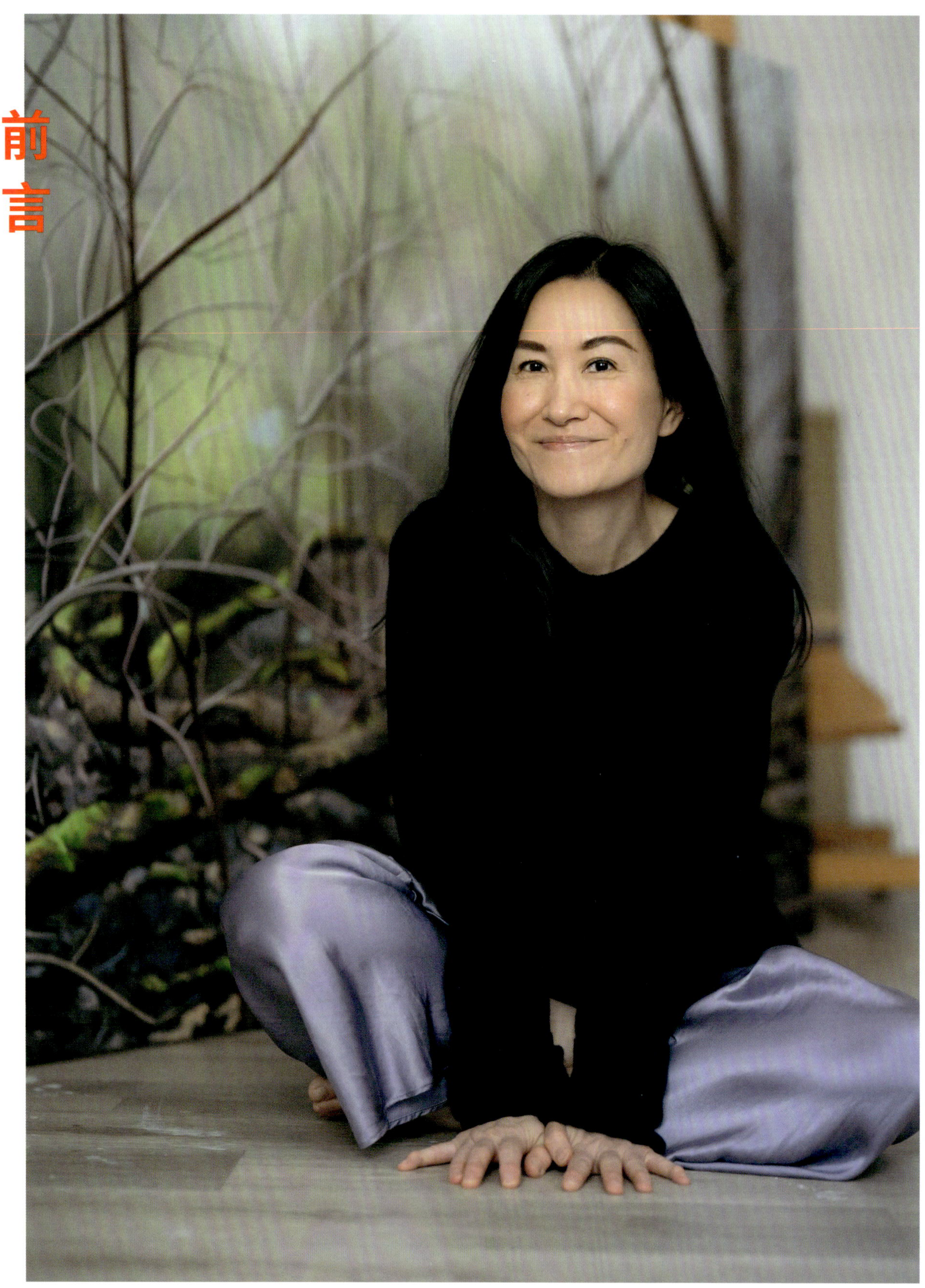

Vorwort
Forword

Seit mehr als 20 Jahren lebt und arbeitet die chinesische Künstlerin Haiying Xu in Deutschland. Obwohl sie die Hälfte ihres bisherigen Lebens in Deutschland verbracht hat, verwendet sie weiterhin ihren chinesischen Namen. Haiying bedeutet auf Deutsch Seeadler, ein Fantasievogel, der kraftvoll über den weiten See fliegen kann. Der Name, den sie bei der Geburt von ihren Eltern erhielt, prophezeite ihr späteres Leben als erwachsene Frau. Sie kam aus dem fernen Osten, wo die Sonne aufgeht, über den Himalaya in den Westen. Diese physische Migration über Tausende von Kilometern erhöht in Xu auf wundersame Weise das Bewusstsein über die kulturelle Bedeutung ihrer Heimat, die die Künstlerin als Gepäck auf den europäischen Kontinent mitgebracht hat. In ihrem Gepäck findet Haiying vor allem ihre Kindheitserinnerungen. In diesem Gepäck ist aber auch die Faszination eines jungen Mädchens für die traditionellen Kulturen ihres Heimatlandes, wie zum Beispiel die aufwendigen und farbenfrohen Masken und Kostüme der Peking-Oper(京剧), die klassische Literatur, die Grottenmalereien aus Dunhuang (敦煌) und die Schattenspiele (皮影戏). Die prächtig gekleideten und aufwendig bemalten Masken der Peking-Oper prägten das ästhetische Empfinden der jungen Haiying. Obwohl zu dieser Zeit immer mehr westliche Kultureinflüsse nach China drangen, träumte sie davon, dieselben Masken und Kostümen in ihrer ganzen Pracht zu tragen: In bodenlangen, farbenprächtigen Kleidern mit geheimnisvollen Symbolen, die auf die Rolle der Figur und ihre Bedeutung in der Geschichte hinwiesen; der üppige Kopfschmuck der Königin, der den ganzen Menschen wie eine blühende Blume erscheinen ließ. Diese Vorstellung von Schönheit wird auch heute noch in der chinesischen Hochzeitskultur praktiziert, indem die Braut einen solchen Kopfschmuck zum Hochzeitsfotoshooting trägt. Auch die dramaturgischen Entwicklungen der literarischen Klassiker aus dem alten China beschäftigen die Künstlerin: Haiying Xu bespielt die Figuren in der großformatigen Szenerie ihres Ölbildes nach eigener Vorstellung. Sie lässt ihrer Fantasie freien Lauf und beleuchtet die zwischenmenschlichen Beziehungen der Figuren, wie sie miteinander interagieren. Diese von ihrer Fantasie veranschaulichte Interaktion macht sichtbar, wie die Künstlerin das Geschehen im Detail beobachtet.

Ihre Malerei von Figuren aus Klassikern der chinesischen Literatur ist nicht als bloße Illustration zu verstehen. Vielmehr konzentriert sich Haiying Xu auf die dramatischen Spannungen zwischen den Figuren und drückt so mit malerischen Mitteln die Spannungen zwischen den Figuren und ihr als beobachtende Zuschauerin aus. Denn ihre ursprüngliche Beziehung zu den literarischen Klassikern war eine bildliche, als sie sie in Form von mangaartigen Bilderbüchern rezipierte, die sie in ihrer Kindheit exzessiv las. In diesen Beziehungen zwischen den Protagonisten und ihrer Betrachterin, die Haiying Xu mit bildnerischen Mitteln artikuliert, werden Problemfelder sichtbar. Wie sähe es aus, wenn sich Tradition und Moderne begegneten. Wenn kulturelle Phänomene, die in der Vergangenheit liegen oder gar in Vergessenheit geraten sind, auf einen modernen Blick träfen, dem diese alte Kultur als fremd und zugleich schön erscheint? Woher käme die Faszination eines Menschen des 21. Jahrhunderts angesichts dieses gigantischen kulturellen Erbes?

Die Werke von Haiying Xu dürfen nicht einzeln betrachtet werden. Jedes Werk ist Fragment eines Ganzen, das sich von Anfang an mit der Frage nach der eigenen Identität beschäftigt.
Aus dieser intensiven Auseinandersetzung entwickelt sich die weitere Sichtweise der deutsch-chinesischen Künstlerin, wie sie die Transformation von Mädchen zu erwachsenen Frauen berührt und ihre Hoffnung für diesen Prozess des Erwachsenwerdens mit bildnerischen Mitteln zum Ausdruck bringt.

Im vorliegenden Katalog sind die Werke in vier Kapiteln gegliedert. Jedes Kapitel steht für eines der künstlerischen Themen, die Haiying Xu seit Beginn ihrer künstlerischen Laufbahn immer wieder aufgegriffen hat. Die zu den jeweiligen Themen gehörenden Werke werden in den jeweiligen Kapiteln chronologisch präsentiert.

Chinese artist Haiying Xu has lived and worked in Germany for over 20 years. Although she has spent half of her life up to now in Germany, she still uses her Chinese name. "Haiying" means "white-tailed eagle" in English, a fantastical bird that has the strength to fly across vast lakes. The name that she was given at birth by her parents prophesized her later life as an adult woman. She came from the far east, where the sun rises, across the Himalayas to the west. This physical migration of thousands of kilometres wondrously heightens Xu's consciousness of the cultural significance of her homeland, which the artist brought with her when she came to Europe. Haiying finds childhood memories in her luggage. She also carries with her a young girl's fascination for the traditional cultures of her homeland, like the intricate and colourful masks and costumes of the Peking opera (京剧), classical literature, cave paintings from Dunhuang (敦煌) and the shadow plays (皮影戏), for instance. The splendidly adorned and painstakingly painted masks of the Peking opera had a big impact on the aesthetic sensibilities of the young Haiying. Although ever-more western influences were forcing their way into China, she dreamed of wearing the same splendid masks and costumes: floor-length, colourful outfits with mysterious symbols that referred to the role of the character and their significance in the story, the queen's luxurious headdress, which gave her the appearance of a flower in bloom. This notion of beauty is still seen in Chinese wedding culture, in which the bride wears the same type of headdress to the wedding photo shoot. The dramaturgical development of the literary classics from ancient China are also on the artist's mind. Haiying Xu depicts the characters as she imagines them to be in the large-format scenery of her oil painting. She lets her imagination run wild and highlights the interpersonal relationships of the characters and how they interact with one another. This illustrated interaction, taken straight from her imagination, shows the artist's eye for detail.

Her paintings of characters from classical Chinese literature are so much more than mere illustration. Haiying Xu is far more concentrated on the dramatic tension between the characters and expresses the tensions between the characters and herself as an observational onlooker in a painterly fashion. Her original relationship with the literary classics was a pictorial one, as she was given them in the form of manga-style picture books, which she read many of in her childhood. Using imagery, Haiying portrays the relationships between the protagonists and their onlooker, thereby making problematic areas visible. What would it look like if tradition and modernity met? What would happen if cultural phenomena, which belong to the past or have even fallen into oblivion, met a modern perspective – someone to whom this old culture seems both strange and simultaneously beautiful? Where did this 21st century person's fascination with this gigantic cultural heritage come from?

The works of Haiying Xu must not be viewed individually. Each work is a fragment of a whole, which, from the very beginning, deals with the question of one's own identity. This intensive examination develops the German-Chinese artist's broader approach, as she touches upon the transformation of girls into adult women and pictorially expresses her hopes for the transition to adulthood.

In the present catalogue the works are divided into four chapters. Each chapter represents an artistic theme, which Haiying Xu has revisited time and time again since the beginning of her artistic career. The works that belong to each topic are presented chronologically in the respective chapters.

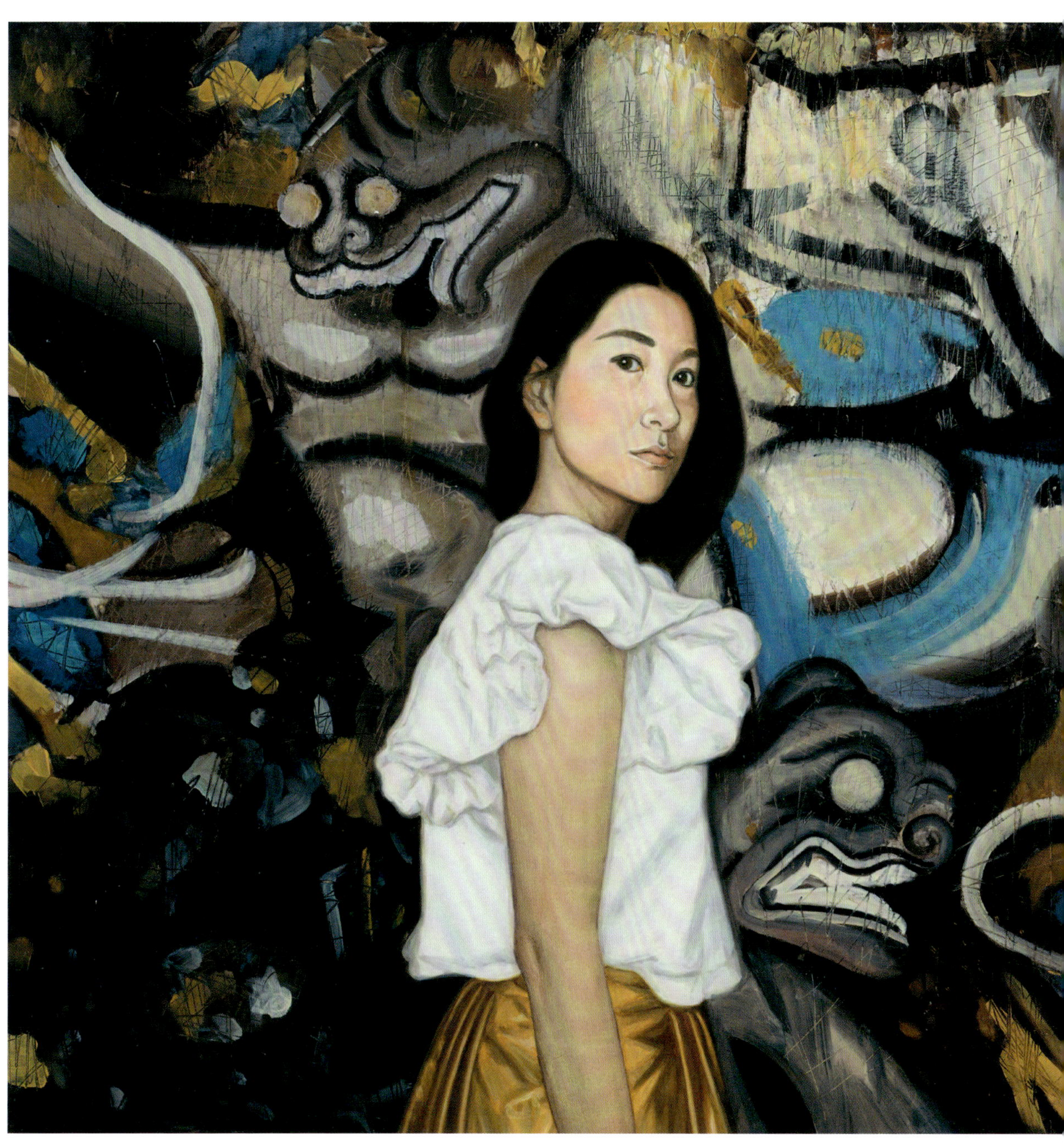

June 2020, 2020
80 x 80 cm
Oil on wood

三百山

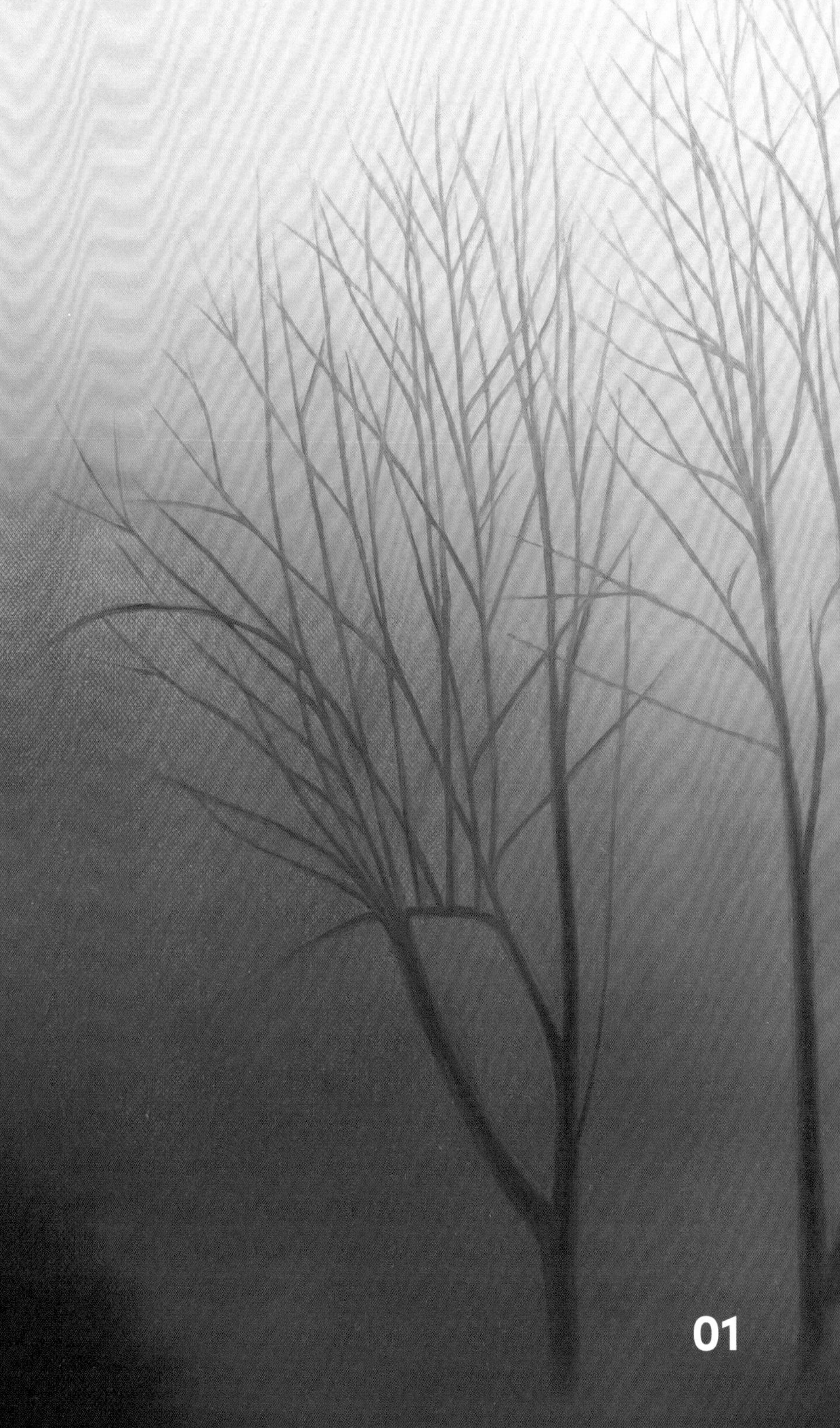

01

Sanbaishan – Dreihundert Berge

Sanbaishan – Three Hundred Mountains

Das Thema Sanbaishan ist die jüngste Entwicklung der deutsch-chinesischen Künstlerin Haiying Xu, dem sie sich seit 2018 intensiv widmet.

Sanbaishan ist ein Ortsname in der Provinz Jiangxi (江西省) in China. Die Provinz Jiangxi liegt im Süden Chinas östlich des Flusses Jangtse (chinesisch Yangzi 扬子江). Der Name Sanbaishan bedeutet „Dreihundert Berge" und repräsentiert offensichtlich nur einen Bruchteil der Berge in dieser Region. Sanbaishan und seine über dreihundert Quadratkilometer große Umgebung sind dicht bewaldet. Die jahrhundertealten Bäume blockieren mit ihren prächtigen Kronen den Himmel und die Sonne. Dadurch bleibt das Klima das ganze Jahr über kühl und angenehm. Sanbaishan vereint vier Naturwunder: Berge, Wälder, Wasserfälle und heiße Quellen präsentieren sich in ihrer Ursprünglichkeit. Im Mai 1993 wurde Sanbaishan vom chinesischen Forstministerium als Nationaler Wildpark anerkannt.

Nach einem längeren Aufenthalt in Deutschland war Sanbaishan für Haiying Xu die erste Station zurück in ihrem Heimatland China. Vier Monate hielt sich Haiying Xu dort mit ihrem kleinen Sohn auf. In dieser Zeit beschäftigte sie sich mit der Frage, wie sie einen Ausweg finden könnte, um von der Mutterrolle wieder in die Künstlerrolle zurückzufinden. Die menschenleere Natur in Sanbaishan eröffnete der Künstlerin einen Raum, in dem sie ihren Lebensweg reflektieren konnte. Die Gedanken und das Dasein in der Natur, die Haiying Xu während ihrer Zeit in Sanbaishan gesammelt hatte, dienten ihr als ideelle Quelle. Aus ihr schuf sie nach ihrer Rückkehr nach Deutschland ihre Bilder mit dem Titel Sanbaishan. Dabei habe der Ort eine wichtige Rolle in Xus Kunst gespielt, so dass auch ihre späteren impressionistischen Walddarstellungen in Lübeck der Sanbaishan-Thematik zugeordnet wurden.

Die thematische Entwicklung aus der Sanbaishan-Zeit kann grob in zwei Phasen unterteilt werden: in der ersten Phase wählte Haiying Xu als Verbindungsträger zwischen Menschen und Natur ein gelbes Boot, in der zweiten und aktuellen Phase ist der Verbindungsträger der Heißluftballon. Große Wasserflächen prägen neben unzähligen hohen Bergen und Wäldern den Ort Sanbaishan. Die Künstlerin identifiziert sich mit den vielfältigen Erscheinungsformen des Elements Wasser. Die klare und ruhige Wasseroberfläche, die mit der umgebenden Landschaft in Spiegelungen interagiert, verbindet die Berge und Wälder miteinander. Der aus dem Wasser aufsteigende Nebel, der der Landschaft einen impressionistischen Charakter verleiht, verbindet die Wahrnehmung der Künstlerin mit der von ihr intensiv studierten traditionellen chinesischen Berg-Wasser-Malerei (中国水墨山水画). Auf den großformatigen Ölgemälden dieses Sanbaishan-Kapitels ist kein Boden zu sehen. In diesem schwebenden Gefühl, mit einem Boot auf dem Wasser zu fahren, das die Künstlerin nach einem Ufer sehnen lässt, scheint das gelbe Boot die einzige Rettung zu sein, um sich im Nebel wieder orientieren zu können. Gelb ist die hellste Farbe in der Farbskala. Ihre Entscheidung, eine leuchtende helle Farbe vor einem düsteren Hintergrundfarbton zu malen, zeigt ihr Bemühen, Hoffnung zu finden. Das Mädchen, das auf dem Bauch liegend mit dem Boot fährt, wirkt sehr entspannt. Ihre Kleidung ist schlicht, das weiße Kleid hebt sich farbig vom dunstigen Hintergrund ab und lenkt so die Aufmerksamkeit des Betrachters auf das Mädchen. Die Künstlerin wählte für ihre Protagonistinnen eine ausdrucksarme Gestik, die die innere Haltung Haiying Xu charakterisiert. Die künstlerische Verarbeitung der Naturstudie von Haiying Xu deutet ihre eigenen Seelenqualitäten an, dass sie für Stimmungen empfänglich ist. Dies ist der Leitgedanke der traditionellen chinesischen Berg-Wasser-Malerei (中国山水画), mit der sich die Künstlerin intensiv auseinandergesetzt hat.

In der zweiten und zugleich aktuellen Schaffensphase zu diesem Thema erhebt Haiying Xu ihren Blick vom Wasser in die Luft. Das Gefühl des Schwebens dramatisiert sich, die konkreten Naturlandschaften abstrahieren sich allmählich ins Dimensionslose, die Protagonistinnen verlassen den Boden und erheben sich in die Luft. Sie scheinen schwerelos zu sein, tanzend wie eine Blume im Wind. Der kühle Farbton ihrer ersten Schaffensphase verwandelt sich in ein Rosa, das es in der Umgebung von Sanbaishan nicht gibt. All diese Veränderungen führen dazu, dass die aktuellen Werke, die Sanbaishan zum Thema haben, surrealistischer geworden sind. In ihrer künstlerisch-geistigen Transformation, in der Haiying Xu versucht, ihre Bilder zu verfremden, möchte sie menschliche Gefühle hervorheben, die rational nicht erklärbar sind. Wie fühlt es sich an, als chinesische Künstlerin in Deutschland zu arbeiten, zu leben. Wie fühlt es sich an, gleichzeitig Mutter und Künstlerin zu sein? Wo liegen die kulturellen Unterschiede weiblicher Identität in Ost und West? Auf dem Weg ihrer persönlichen Suche nach Antworten entdeckt sie die Dimension des Unbewussten, die wir in unseren Schatten verdrängt haben, weil wir uns im alltäglichen Umgang mit unseren Mitmenschen bewusst oder unbewusst vor allem um ein perfektes Selbstbild bemühen, das der gesellschaftlichen Norm entspricht.

Vor dieser Intention kann man die tanzenden Mädchen, die in der rosafarbenen Luft schweben, als Göttin der Befreiung lesen, die an die Figuren der Feitian（飞天）aus der Dunghuang-Kultur（敦煌文化）erinnern, von wo aus sich der Buddhismus in ganz China zu verbreiten begann. Die Feitian sind kleine Göttinnen, die weiblich aussehen und durch die Lüfte fliegen, um das Paradies zu feiern. Im Grunde schafft Haiying Xu Bilder, die von ihrer Intuition geleitet werden. Eine Künstlerin, die die Stimmung malt, wie sie auf ihre Außenwelt reagiert und so in Beziehung zu ihrer eigenen Intuition tritt. Ihr künstlerischer Ausdruck ist daher zärtlich, lieblich, ungezwungen, gelöst und frei. In ihrem künstlerischen Ausdruck kann man ihren selbstkritischen Blick rezipieren, der die Künstlerin Haiying Xu in ihrer ästhetischen Formulierung zu dem Weg der Selbstanerkennung führt.

The theme "Sanbaishan" is the most recent development of the German-Chinese artist Haiying Xu, which she has intensely dedicated herself to since 2018.

Sanbaishan is the name of a place in the province of Jiangxi（江西省）in China. The province of Jiangxi is situated in southern China, east of the Yangtze River (Chinese: Yangzi 扬子江). The name Sanbaishan means "three hundred mountains" and clearly only represents a small portion of the mountains in this region. Sanbaishan and the surrounding area, comprising over three hundred square kilometres, is covered in dense woodland. That's why the climate remains cool and pleasant there the whole year around. Sanbaishan brings together four natural wonders: untouched mountains, forests, waterfalls and hot springs are all present. In May 1993 Sanbaishan was recognized as a national wildlife park by the Chinese National Forestry and Grassland Administration.

Having resided in Germany for a long time, Haiying Xu's first stop back in her home country was Sanbaishan. Haiying Xu spent four months there with her young son. During this time, she asked herself how she could find a way out of the role of the mother back to the role of the artist. Sanbaishan's uninhabited natural environment allowed the artist space to reflect upon her life path. The thoughts Haiying Xu gathered and her presence in nature during her time in Sanbaishan served as a source of new ideas. This source led her to create a series of pictures entitled Sanbaishan after her return to Germany. The place played an important role in Xu's art, so much so that even her later impressionist depictions of forests in Lübeck were categorized under the thematic title of Sanbaishan.

The thematic evolution that emerged from Xu's time in Sanbaishan can roughly be divided into two phases. In the first phase, Haiying Xu chose a yellow boat to function as a connection between people and nature. In the second and current phase, this connection is a hot-air balloon. Great bodies of water, along with countless high mountains and forests shape Sanbaishan. The artist identifies with the various manifestations of the element of water. The clear and quiet surface of the water, which interacts with the surrounding landscape by means of reflections, connects the mountains and the forests with one another. The rising mist emerging from the water lends the landscape an impressionist quality, connecting the artist's perception with that seen in traditional Chinese paintings of mountains and water（中国水墨山水画）, which she has studied intensively. The ground cannot be seen in the large-format oil paintings of the Sanbaishan chapter. This floating sensation of travelling by boat makes the artist long for the riverbank, making the yellow boat appear to be the only salvation by which to navigate in the fog once again. Yellow is the lightest colour in the spectrum of colours. Her decision to use a glowing, bright colour against a dark background shade shows her effort to find hope. The girl, who is lying on her front and travelling on board the boat, looks very relaxed. Her clothing is unpretentious. The colour of the white dress is a stark contrast to the hazy background and directs the onlooker's attention to the girl. The artist chose to have her female protagonists gesticulate expressively, characterizing Haiying Xu's intrinsic attitude. The artistic workmanship of Haiying Xu's study of nature hints at her own soulful qualities and her receptivity to different atmospheres. This is the guiding thread in traditional Chinese paintings of mountains and water(中国山水画), which the artist has studied in great detail.

In the second and also the contemporary phase of the artist's creative output in connection to this topic, Haiying Xu lifts her gaze from the water to the air. The sensation of floating is dramatized. Specific landscapes gradually become abstract and lose all sense of dimension. The protagonists leave the ground and rise up into the air. They seem to be weightless, dancing like a flower in the wind. The cool shade of her first creative phase transforms into a shade of pink, which does not exist in the surroundings of Sanbaishan. All these changes mean that the latest works depicting Sanbaishan have become more surreal. In her artistic, spiritual transformation, through which Haiying Xu attempts to make her pictures appear unfamiliar, she highlights human feelings that cannot be rationally explained. How does it feel to work and live as a Chinese artist in Germany? How does it feel to simultaneously be a mother and an artist? Where are the cultural differences between female identity in the East and the West? While on her own personal quest for answers, she discovers the dimension of the unconscious, which we have repressed in our shadow, because in day-to-day interactions with other people, we consciously or often unconsciously make efforts to portray a perfect version of ourselves that corresponds to the social norm.

With this intention in mind, the dancing girls, who are floating in the pink-coloured air can be seen as goddesses of liberation. They are reminiscent of the characters in Feitian(飞天), taken from Dunghuang culture, the starting point from where Buddhism began to spread throughout the whole of China. The Feitian are small goddesses that look female and fly through the skies to celebrate paradise. In principle, Haiying Xu's intuition guides her when she is creating images. She is an artist who paints the mood with which she reacts to the outside world, and thus how she relates to her own intuition. Her self-critical view is tangible in her artistic expression, which through aesthetic form, leads the artist Haiying Xu along the path to self-recognition.

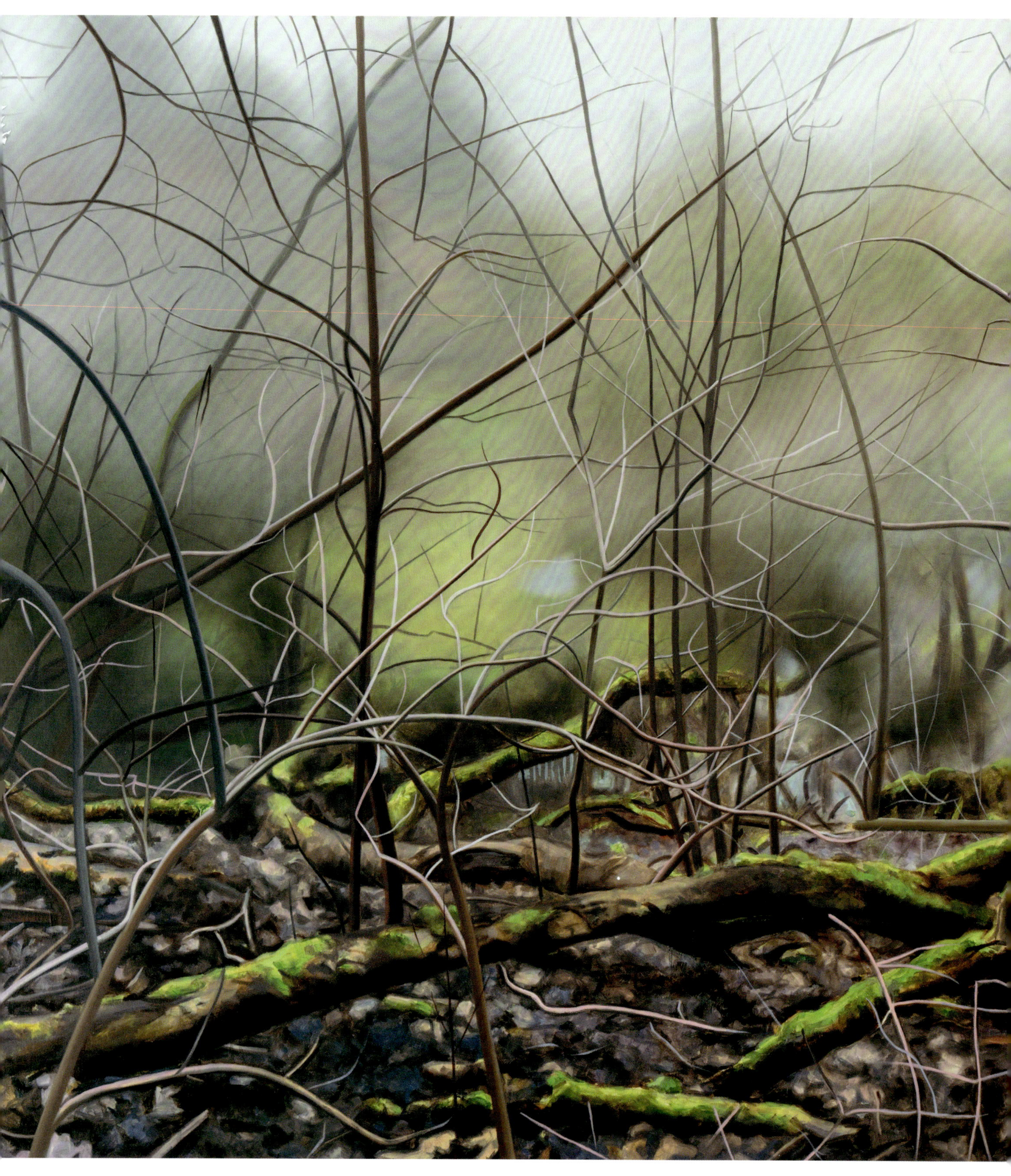

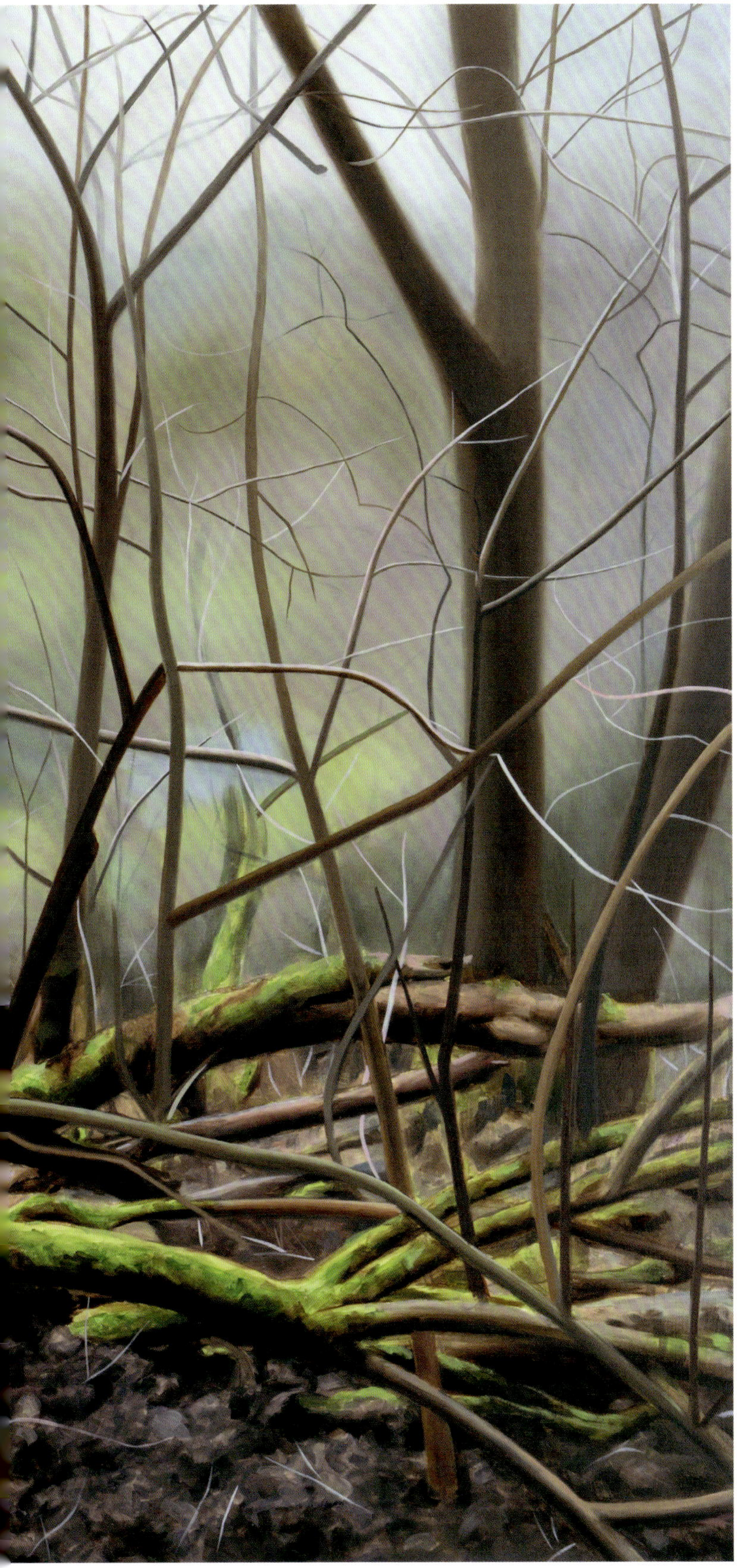

Once Upon a Time 16, 2023
130 x 190 cm
Oil on canvas

Once Upon a Time 17, 2023
190 x 130 cm
Oil on canvas

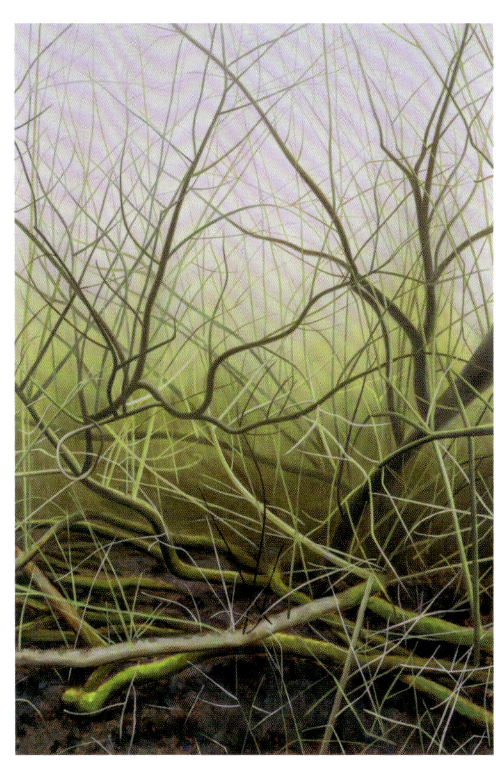

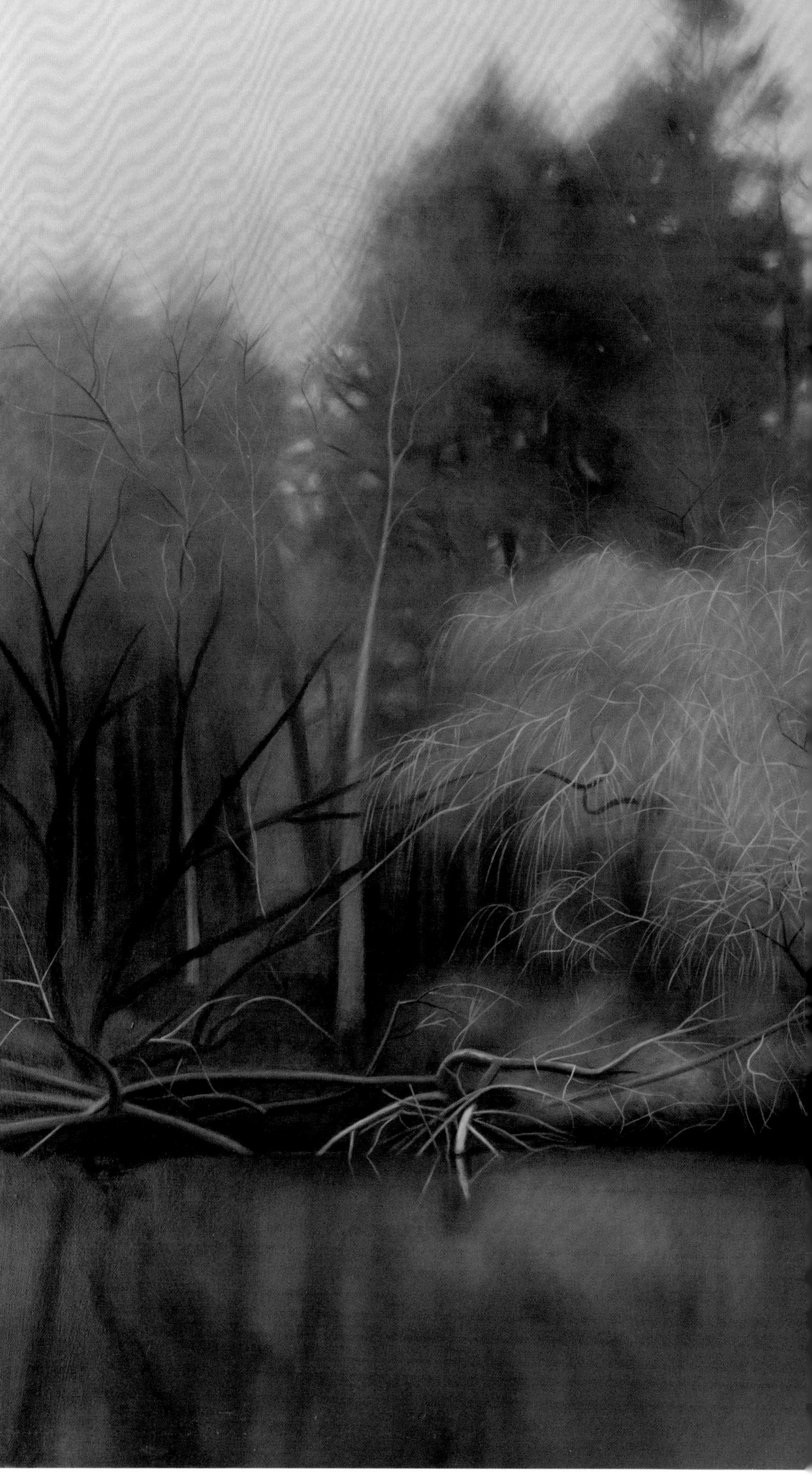

Once Upon a Time 15, 2023
130 x 190 cm
Oil on canvas

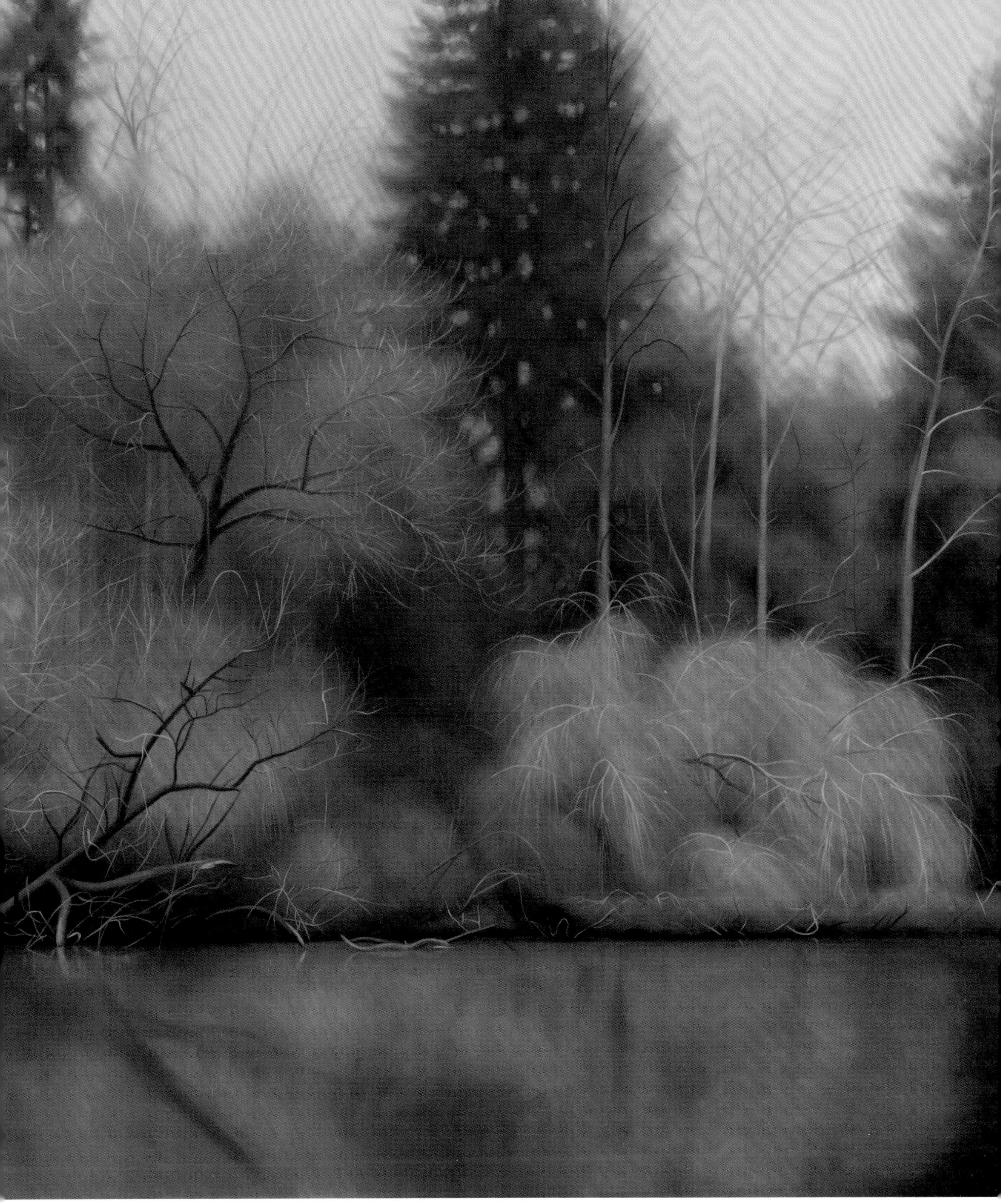

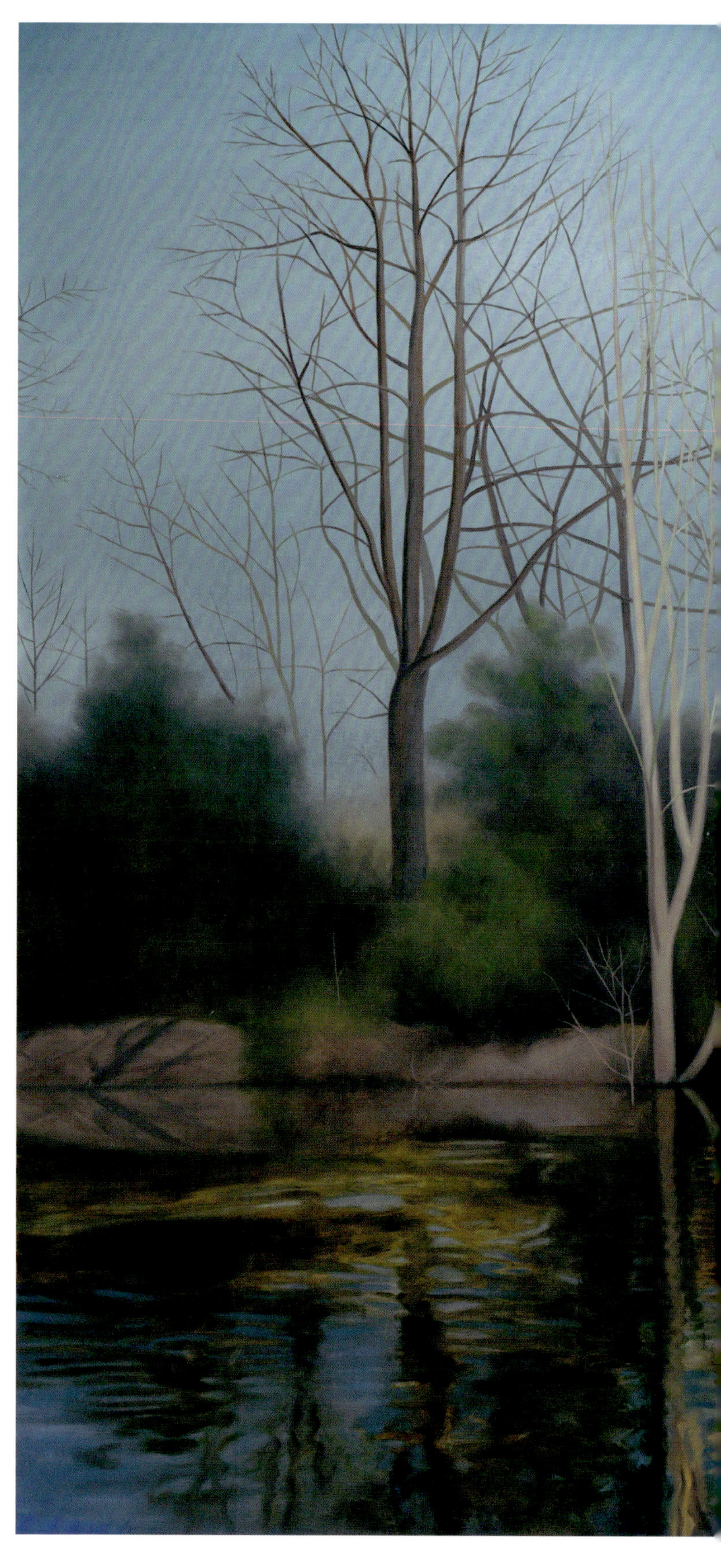

The Journey 14, 2022
130 x 190 cm
Oil on canvas

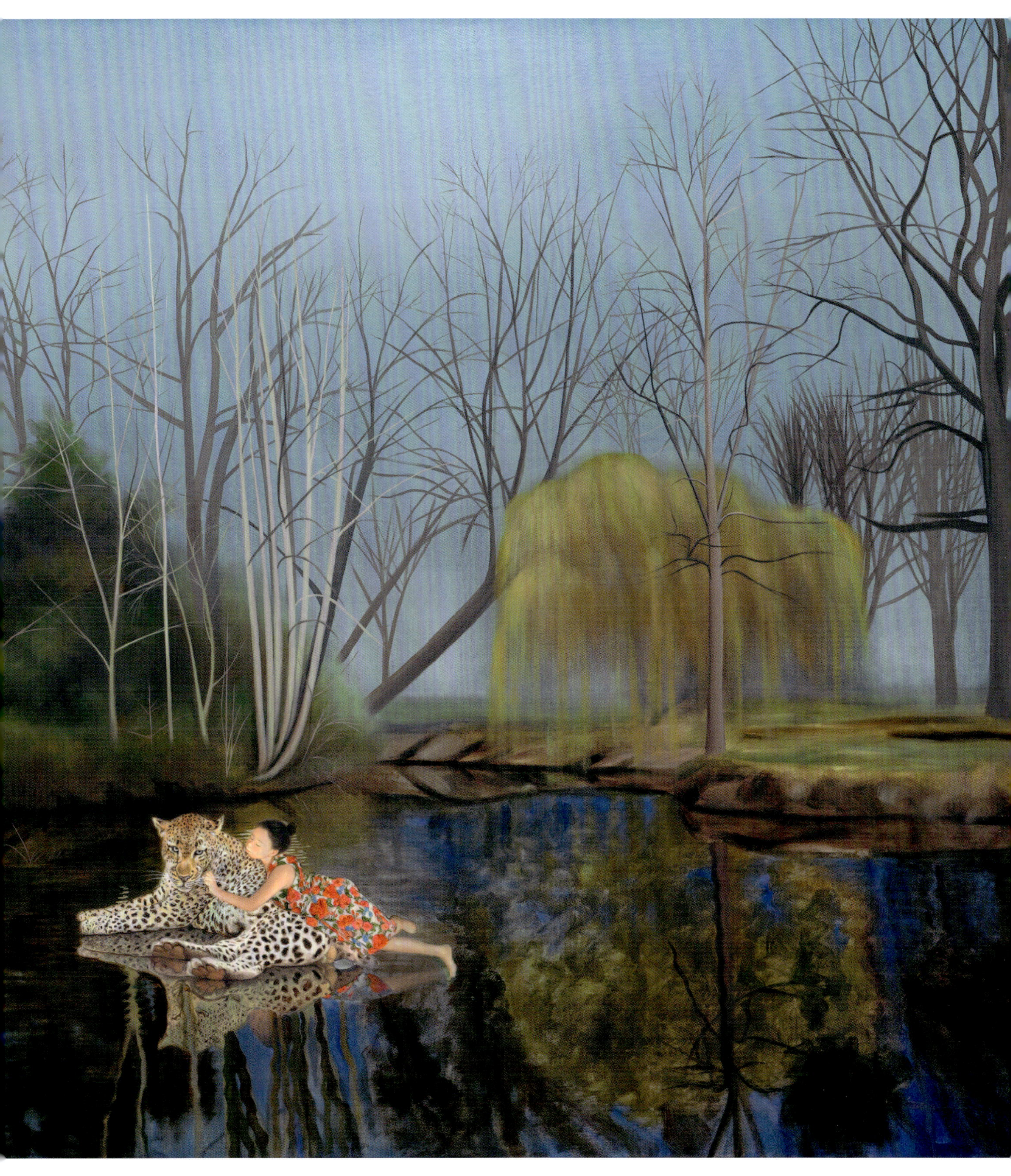

Sanbaishan 12, 2021
150 x 110 cm
Oil on canvas

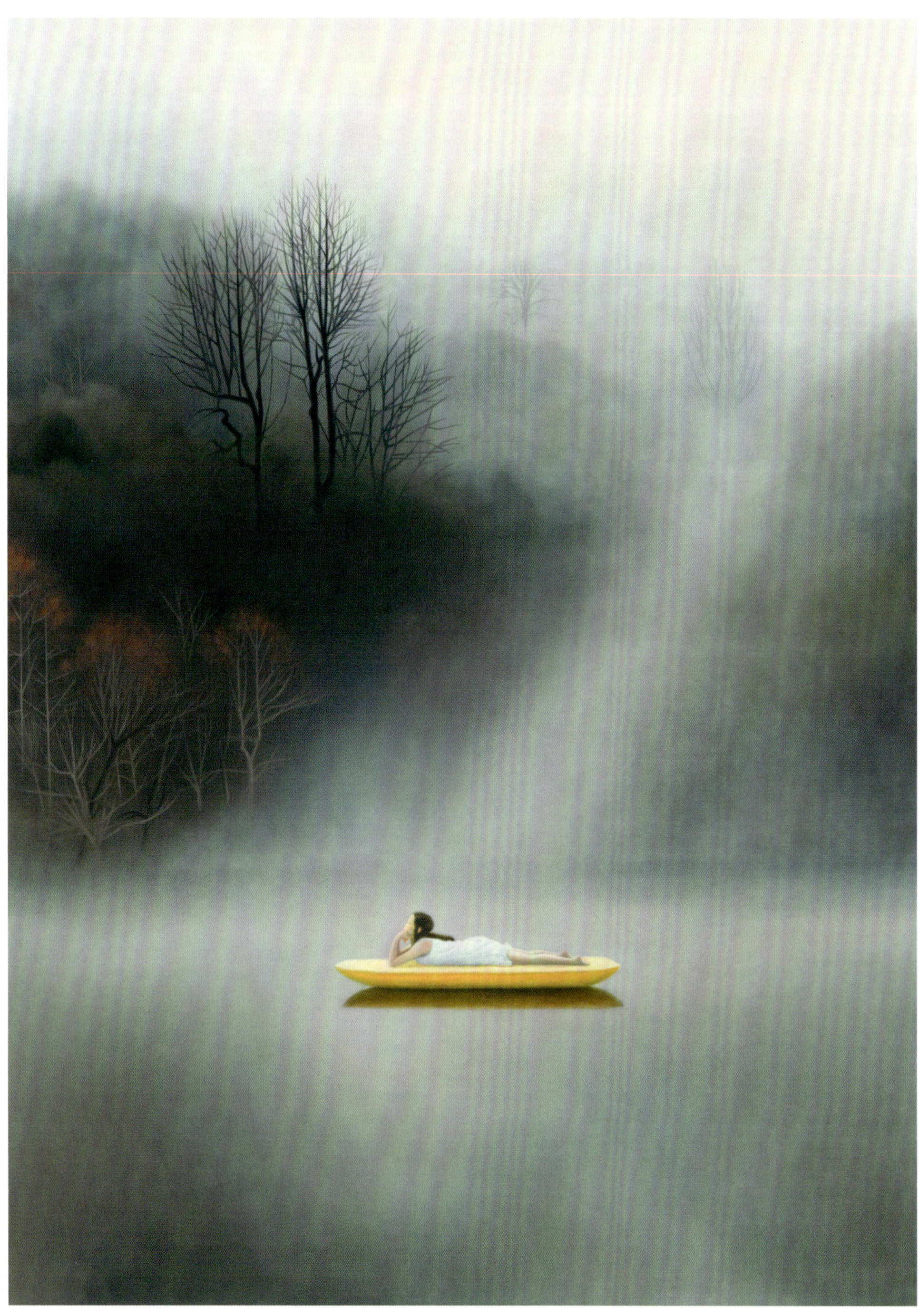

Sanbaishan 18, 2022
120 x 90 cm
Oil on canvas

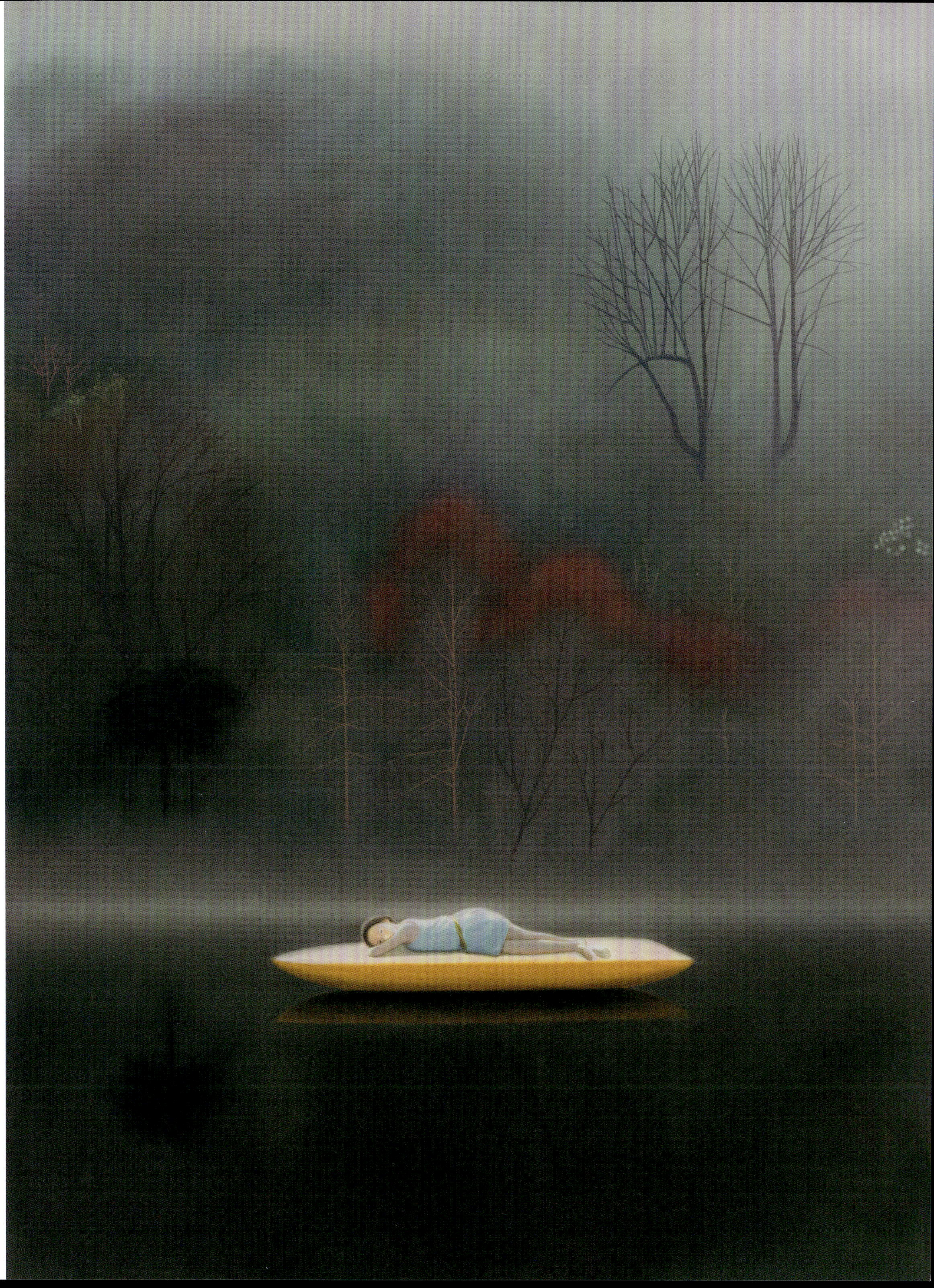

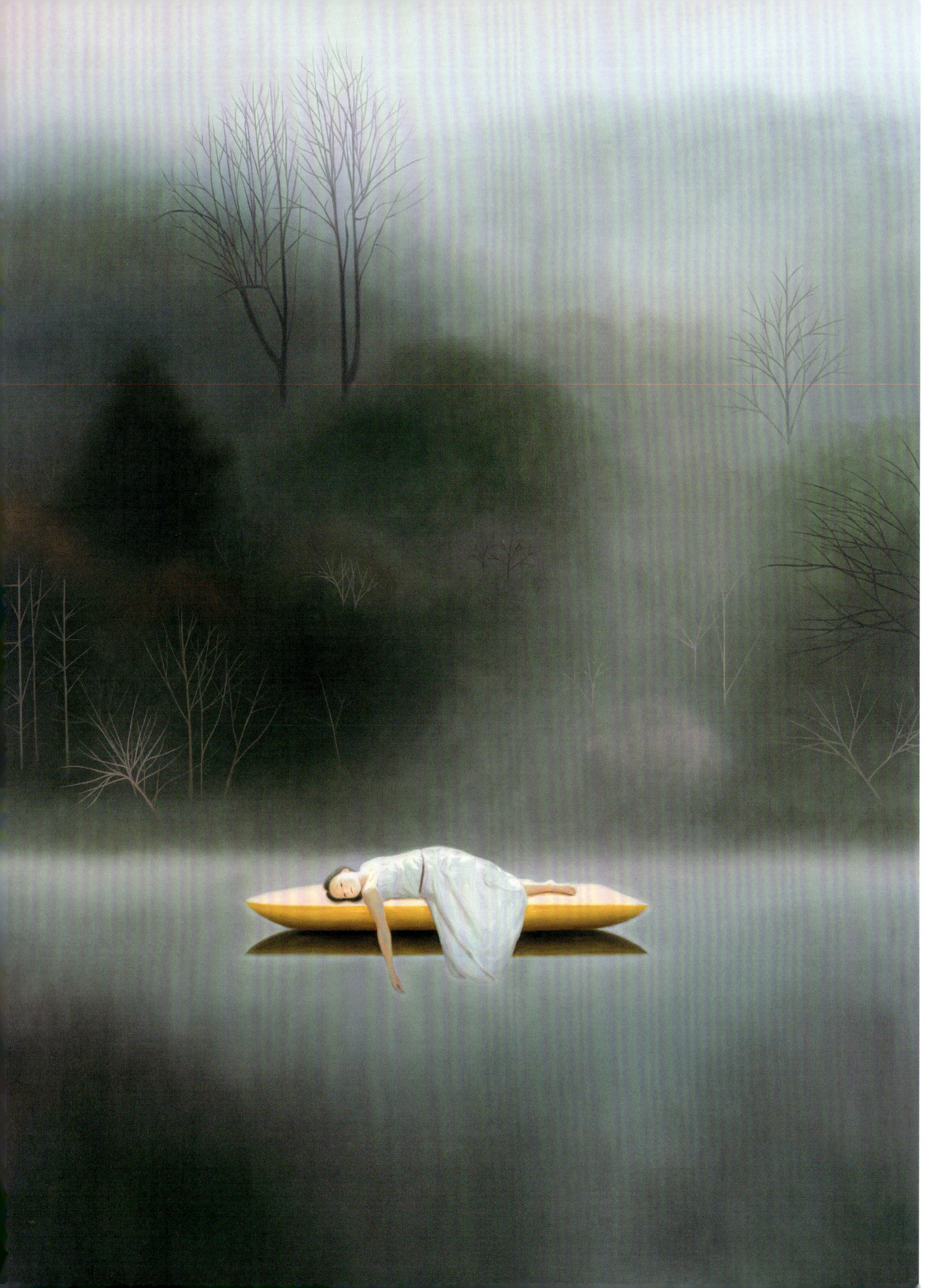

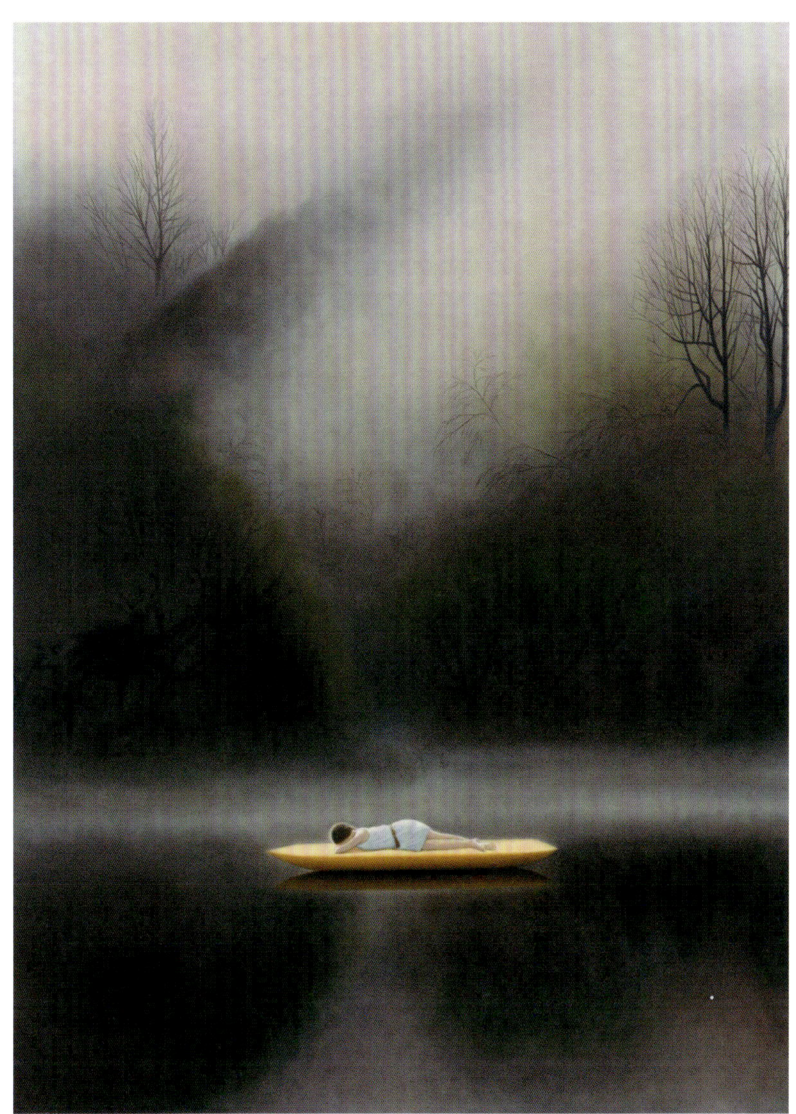

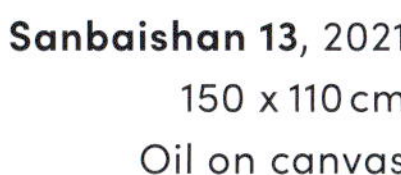

Sanbaishan 13, 2021
150 x 110 cm
Oil on canvas

Sanbaishan 08, 2021
70 x 50 cm
Oil on wood

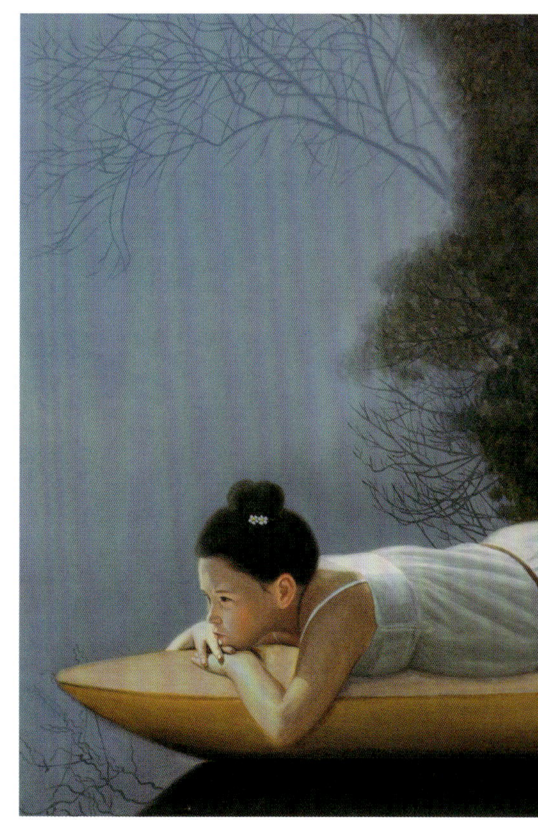

Sanbaishan 19, 2022
150 x 110 cm
Oil on canvas

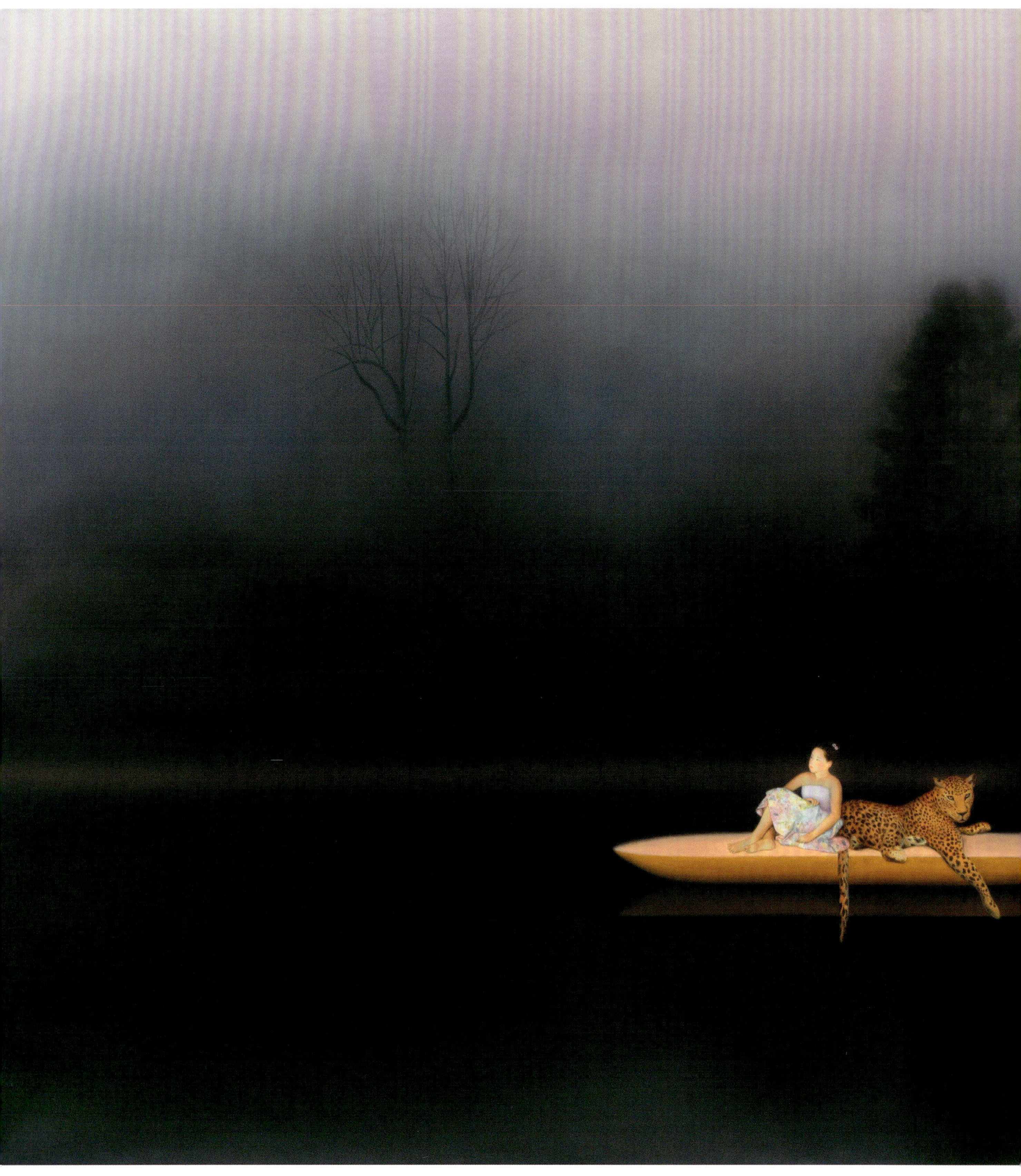

Sanbaishan 22, 2022
130 x 190 cm
Oil on canvas

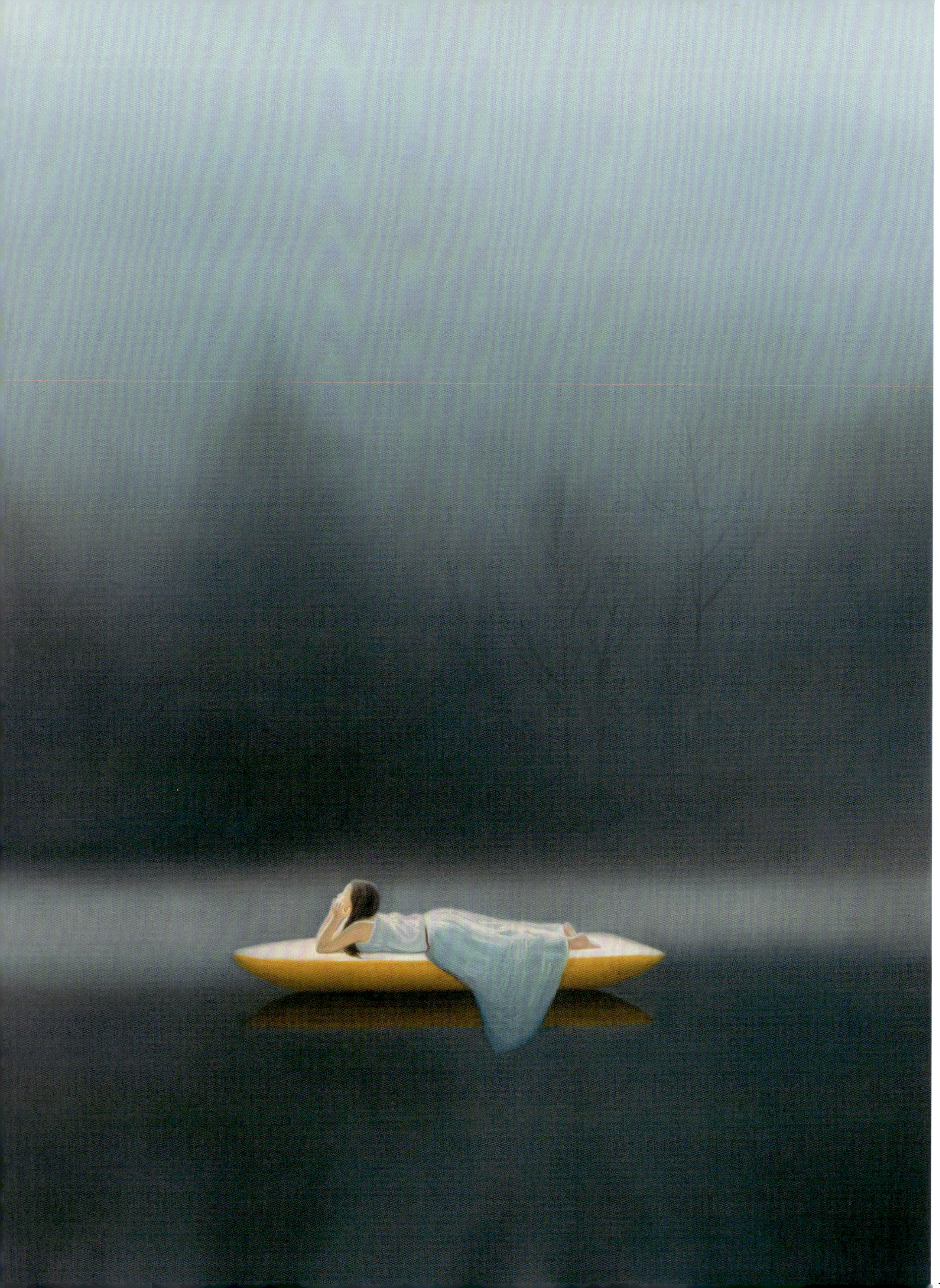

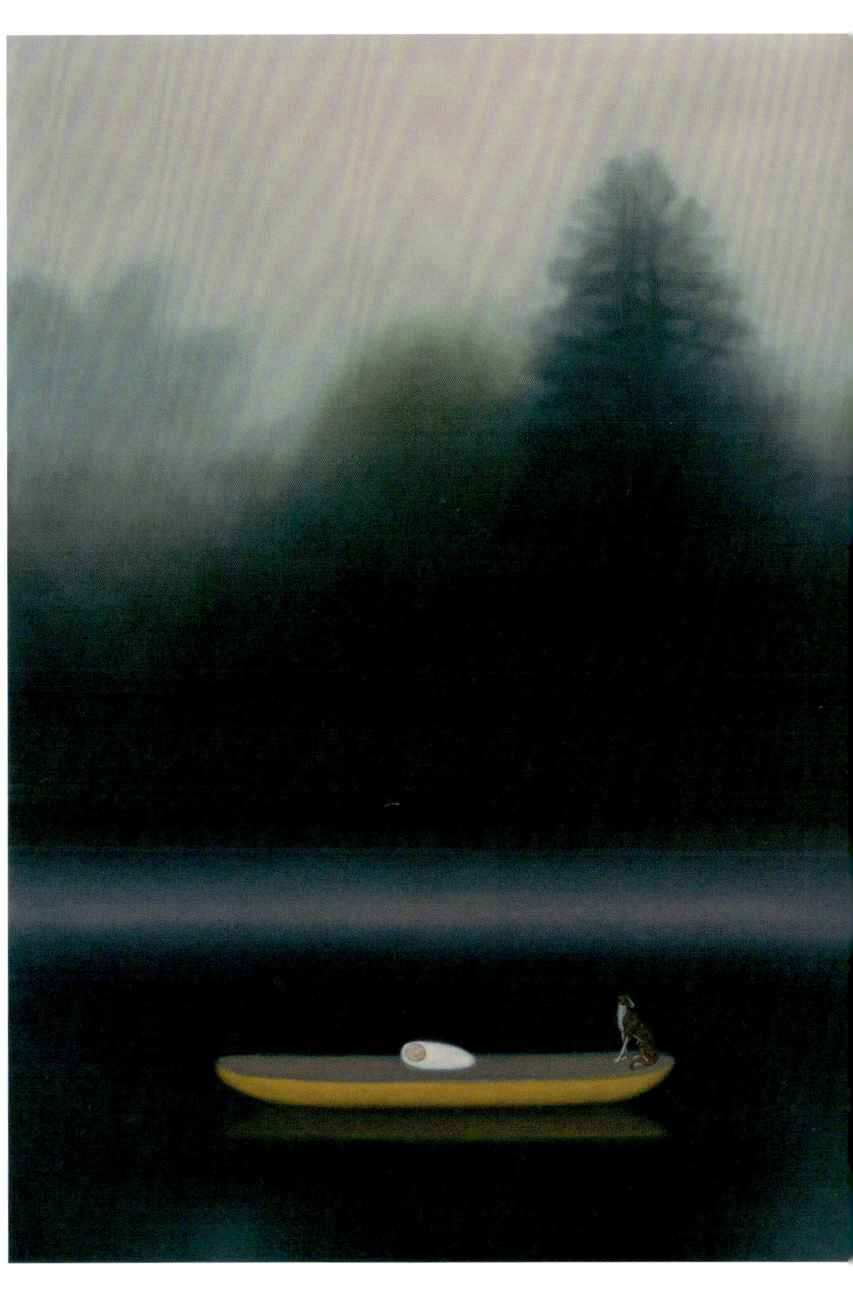

Sanbaishan 17, 2022
120 x 90 cm
Oil on canvas

Sanbaishan 11, 2020
100 x 70 cm
Oil on canvas

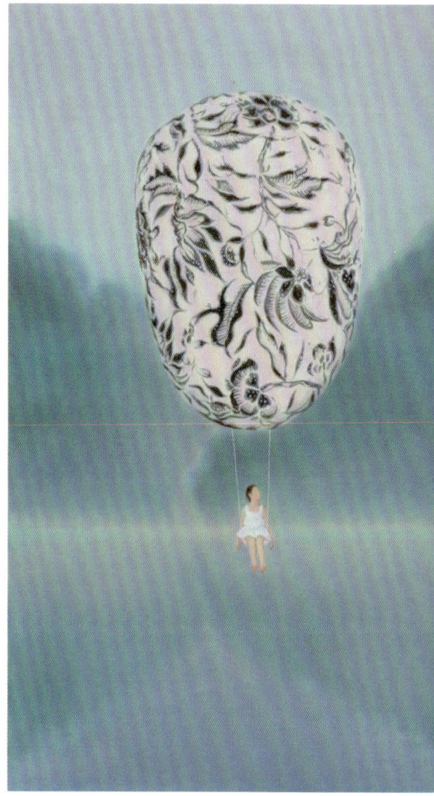

Sanbaishan 28, 2023
100 x 80 cm
Oil on canvas

Sanbaishan 27, 2023
80 x 50 cm
Oil on canvas

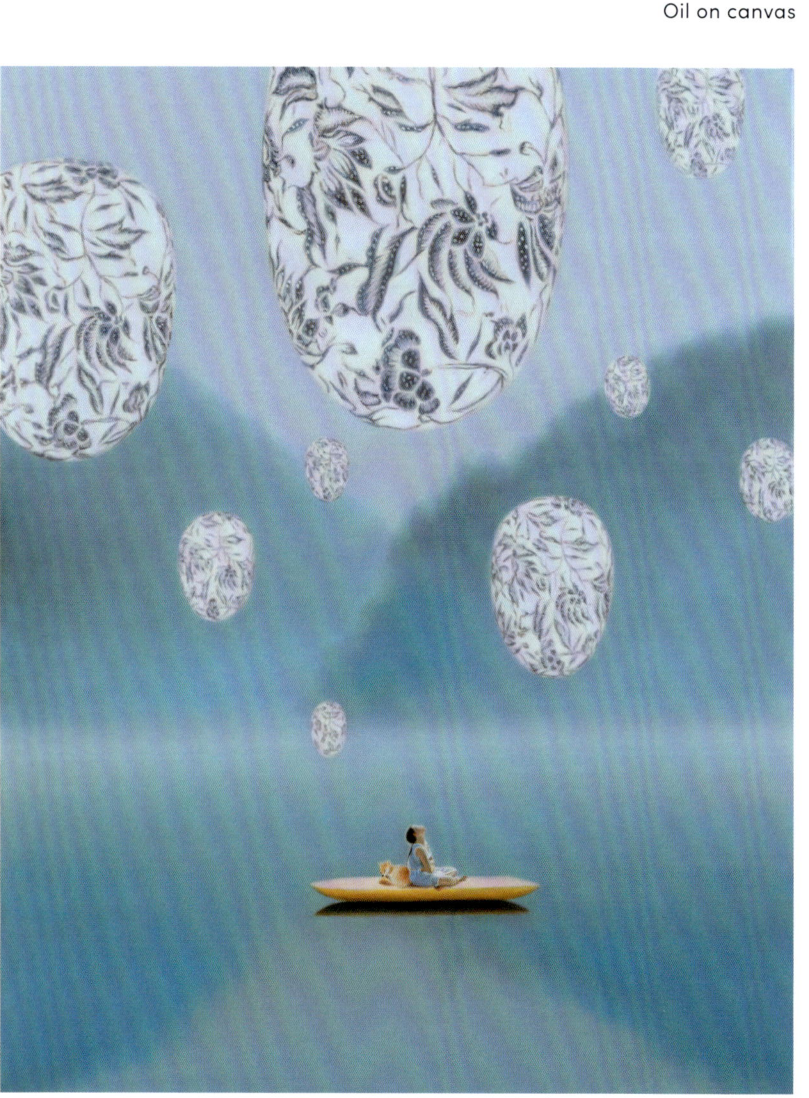

Sanbaishan 25, 2023
190 x 130 cm
Oil on canvas

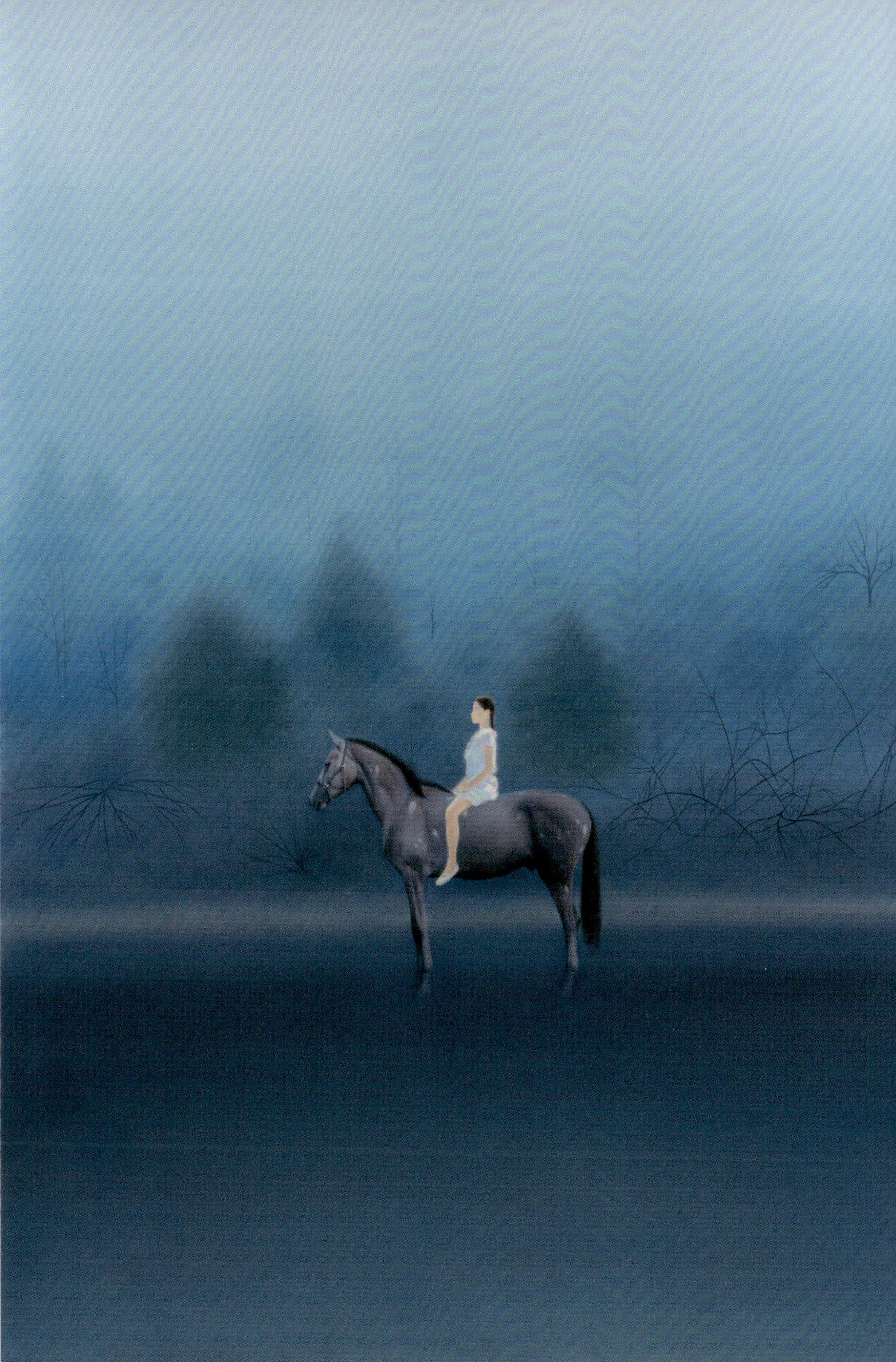

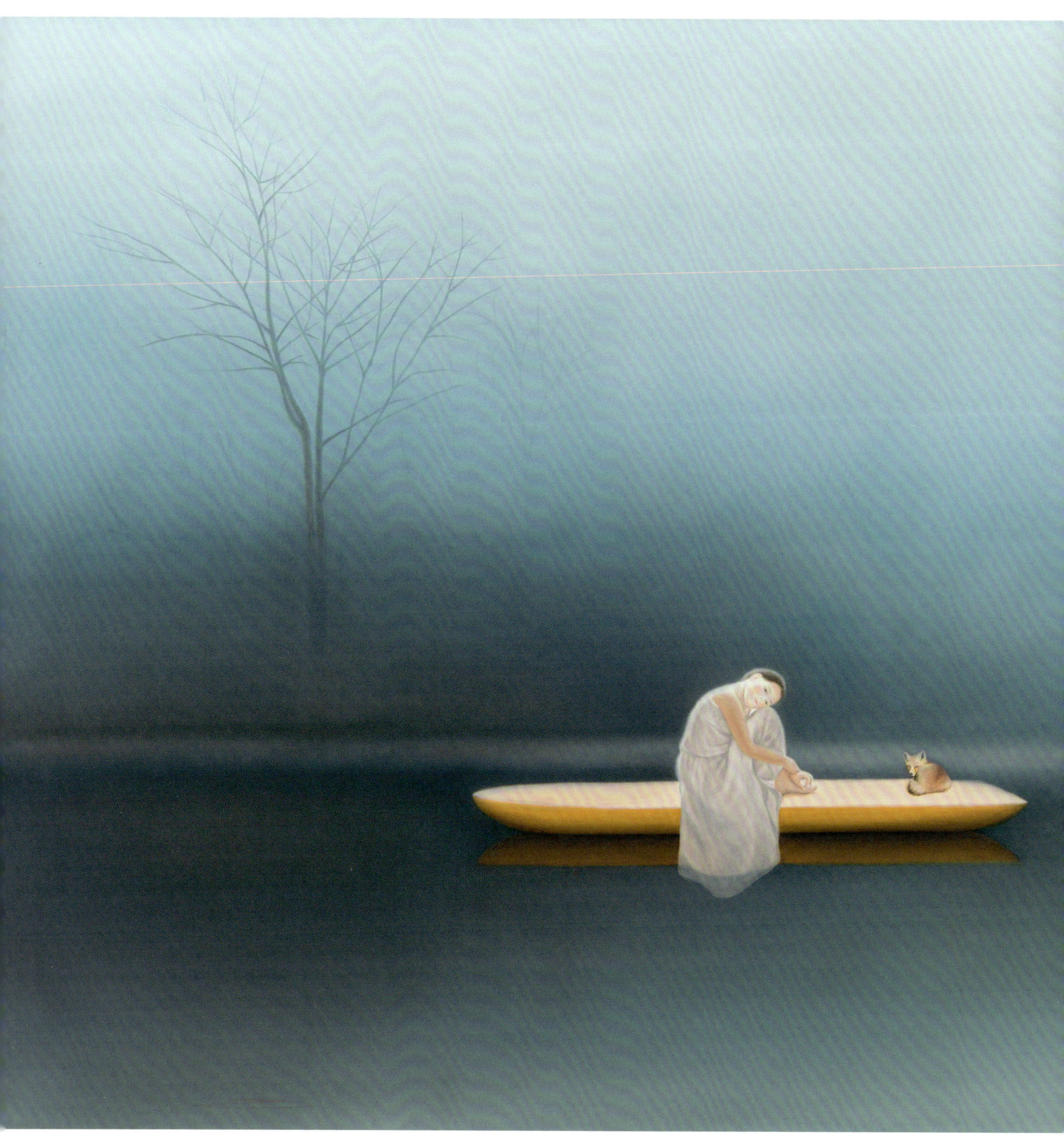

Sanbaishan 16, 2022
110 x 150 cm
Oil on canvas

Sanbaishan 07, 2018
100 x 160 cm
Oil on canvas

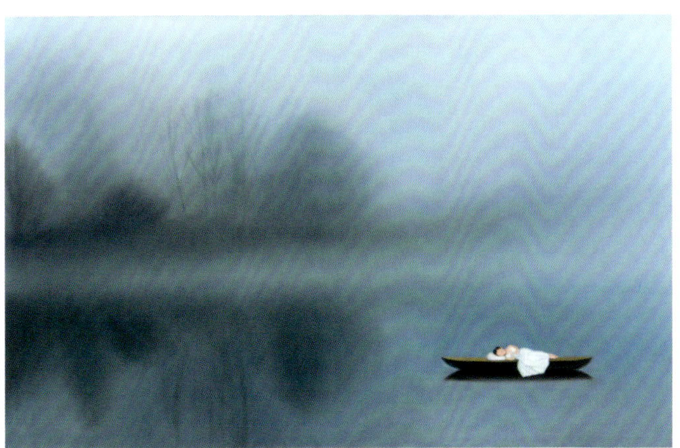

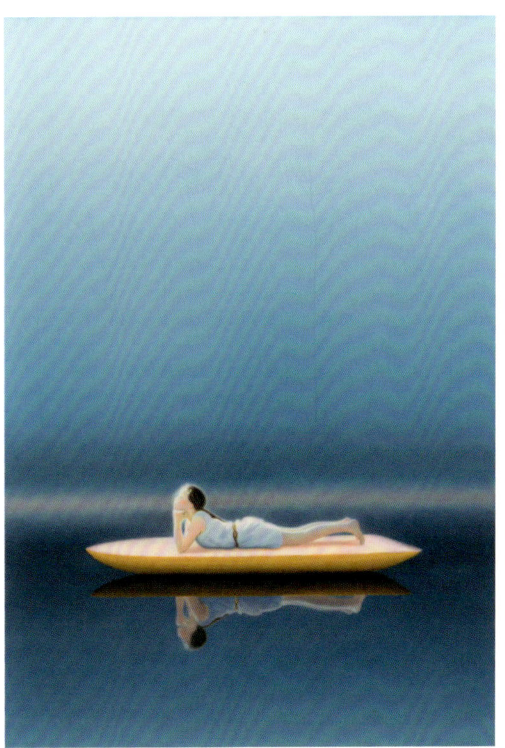

Sanbaishan 23, 2022
100 x 70 cm
Oil on canvas

Sanbaishan 09, 2020
100 x 70 cm
Oil on canvas

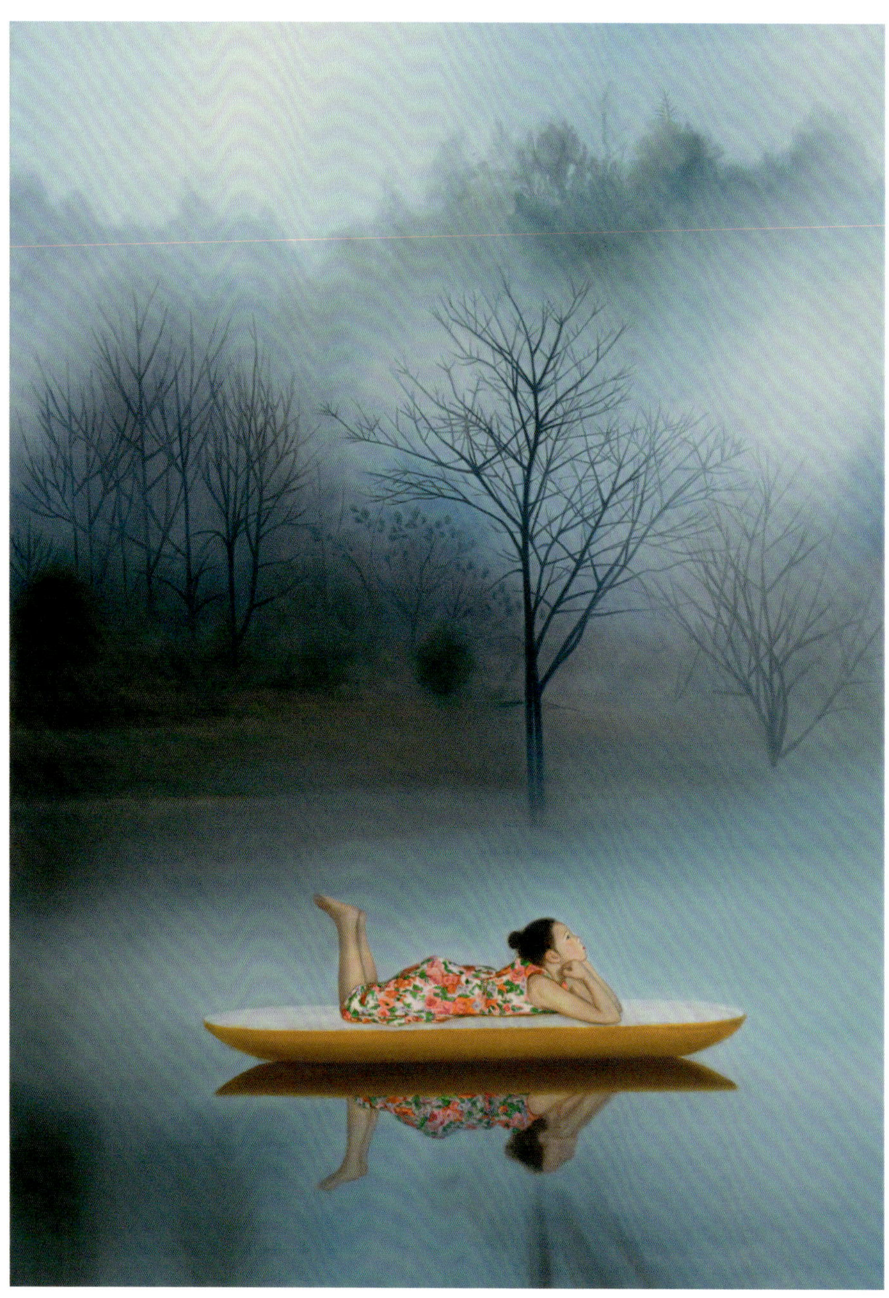

Sanbaishan 10, 2020
100 x 70 cm
Oil on canvas

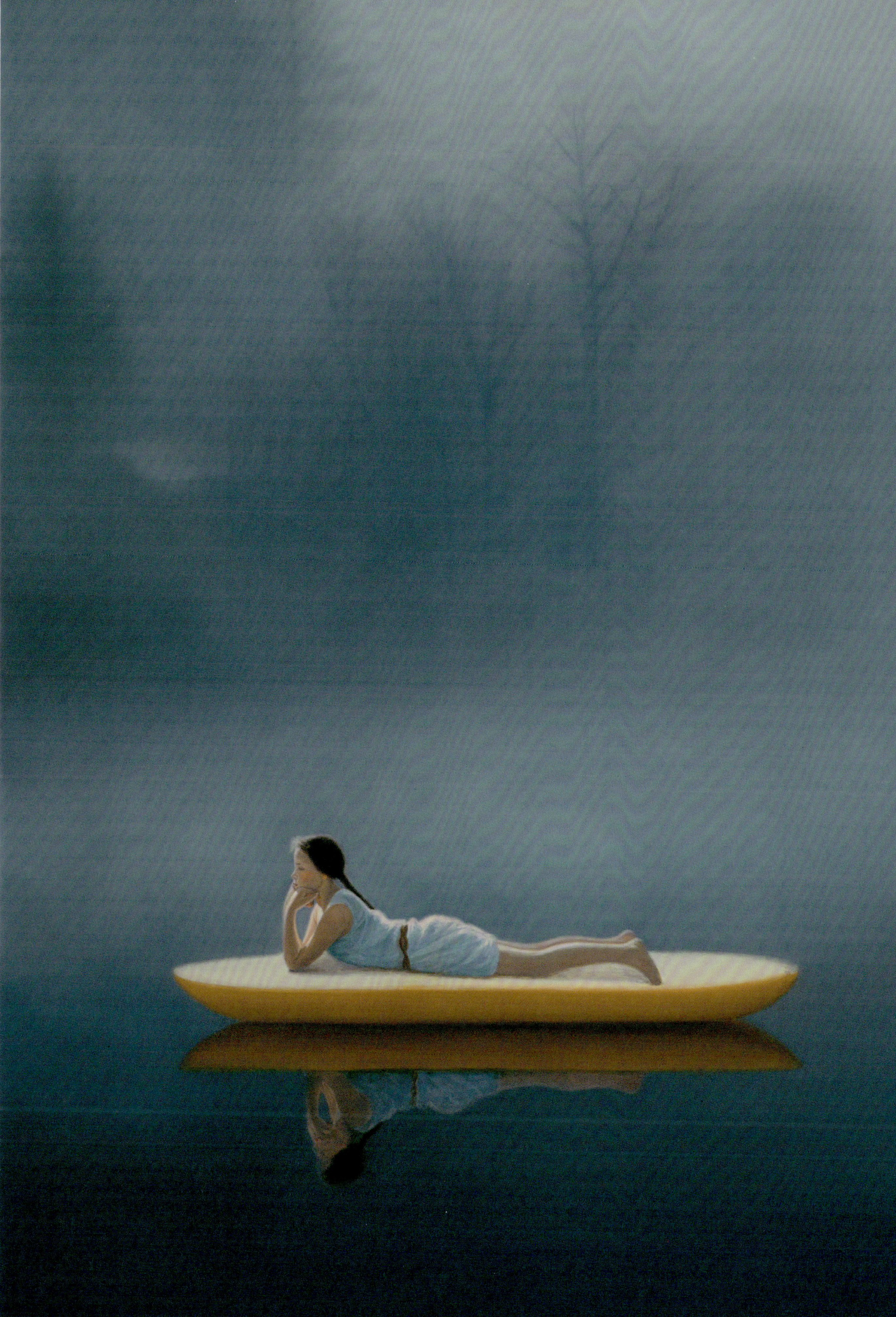

Sanbaishan 24, 2022
70 x 100 cm
Oil on canvas

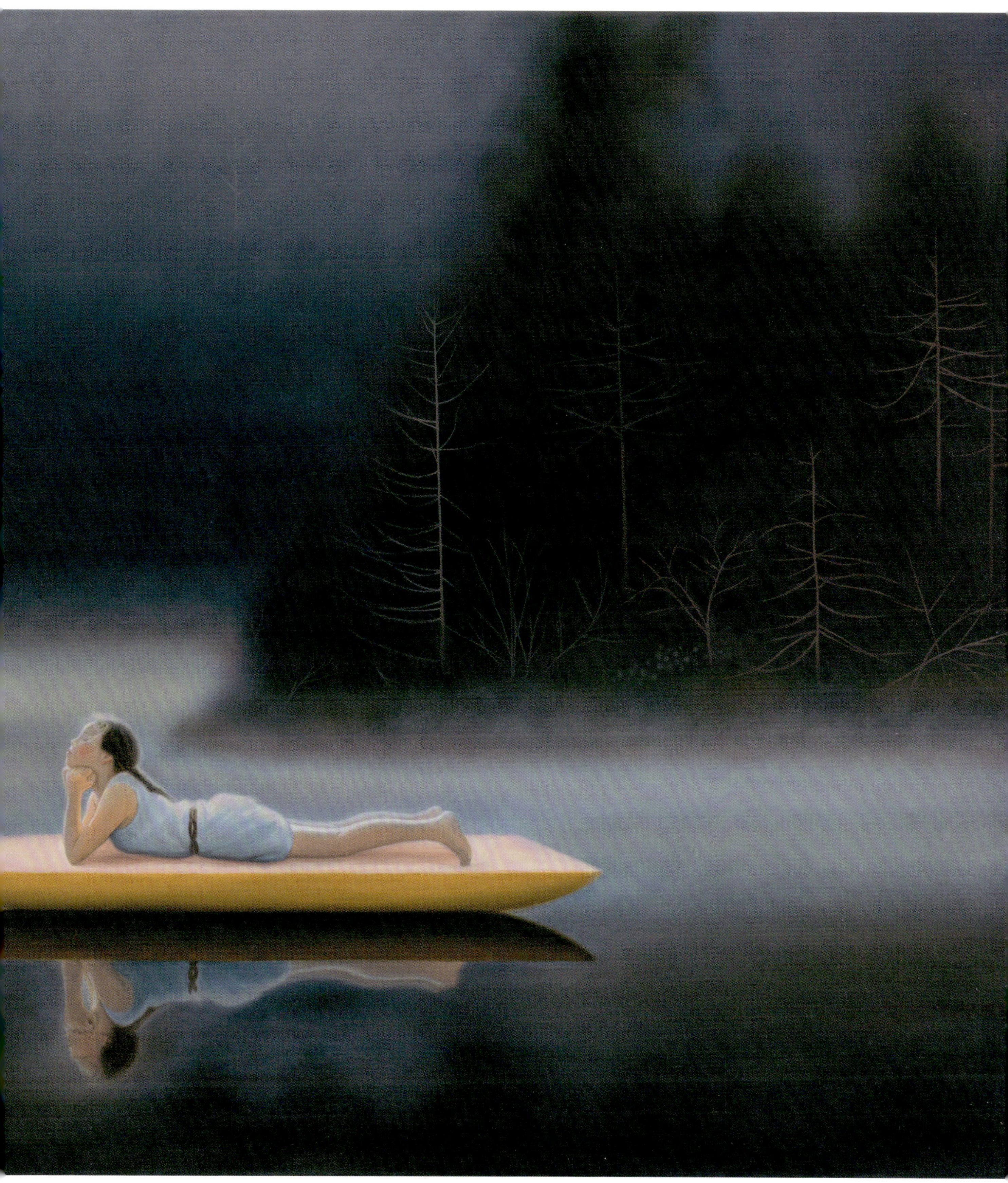

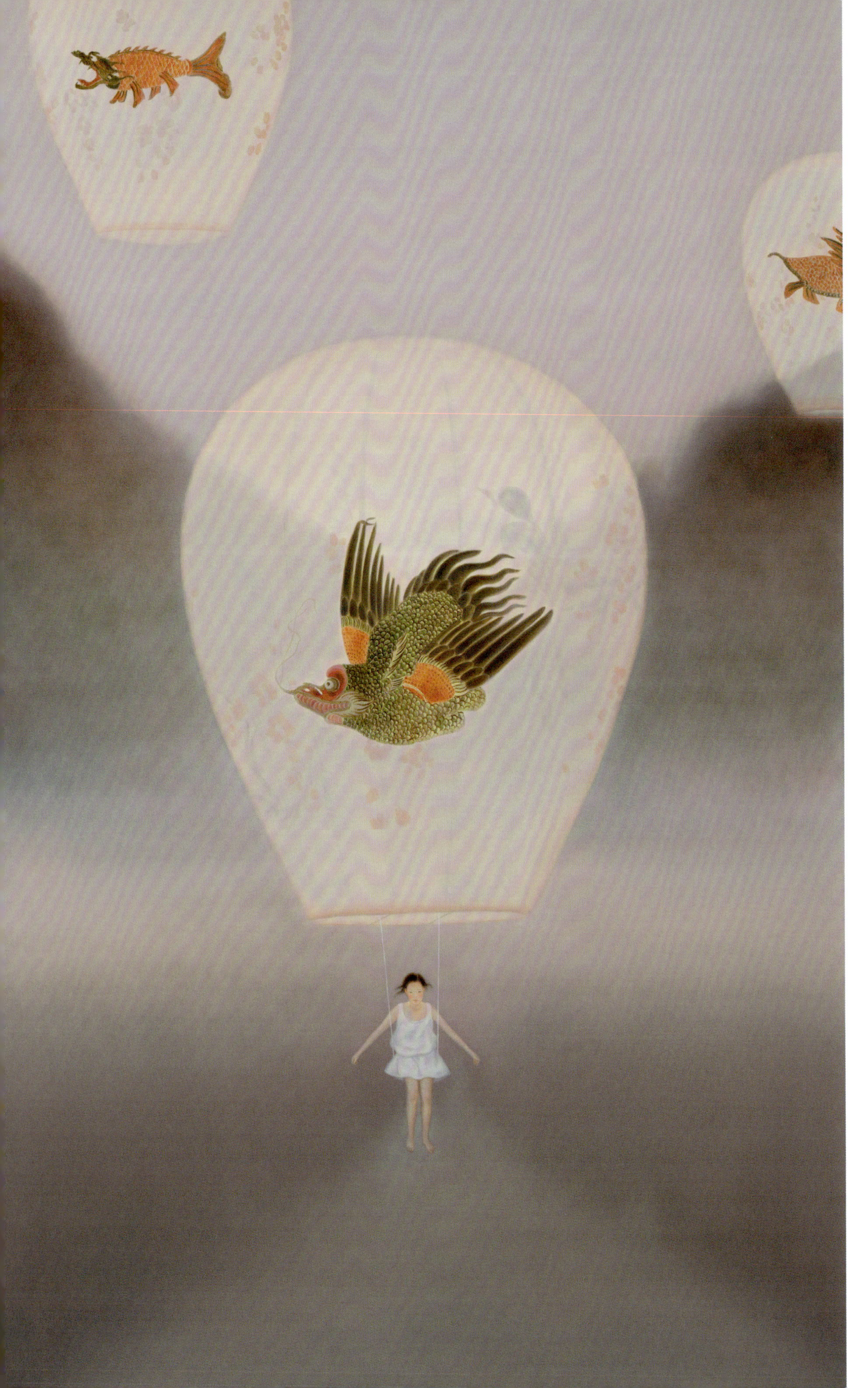

Sanbaishan 29, 2023
160 x 100 cm
Oil on canvas

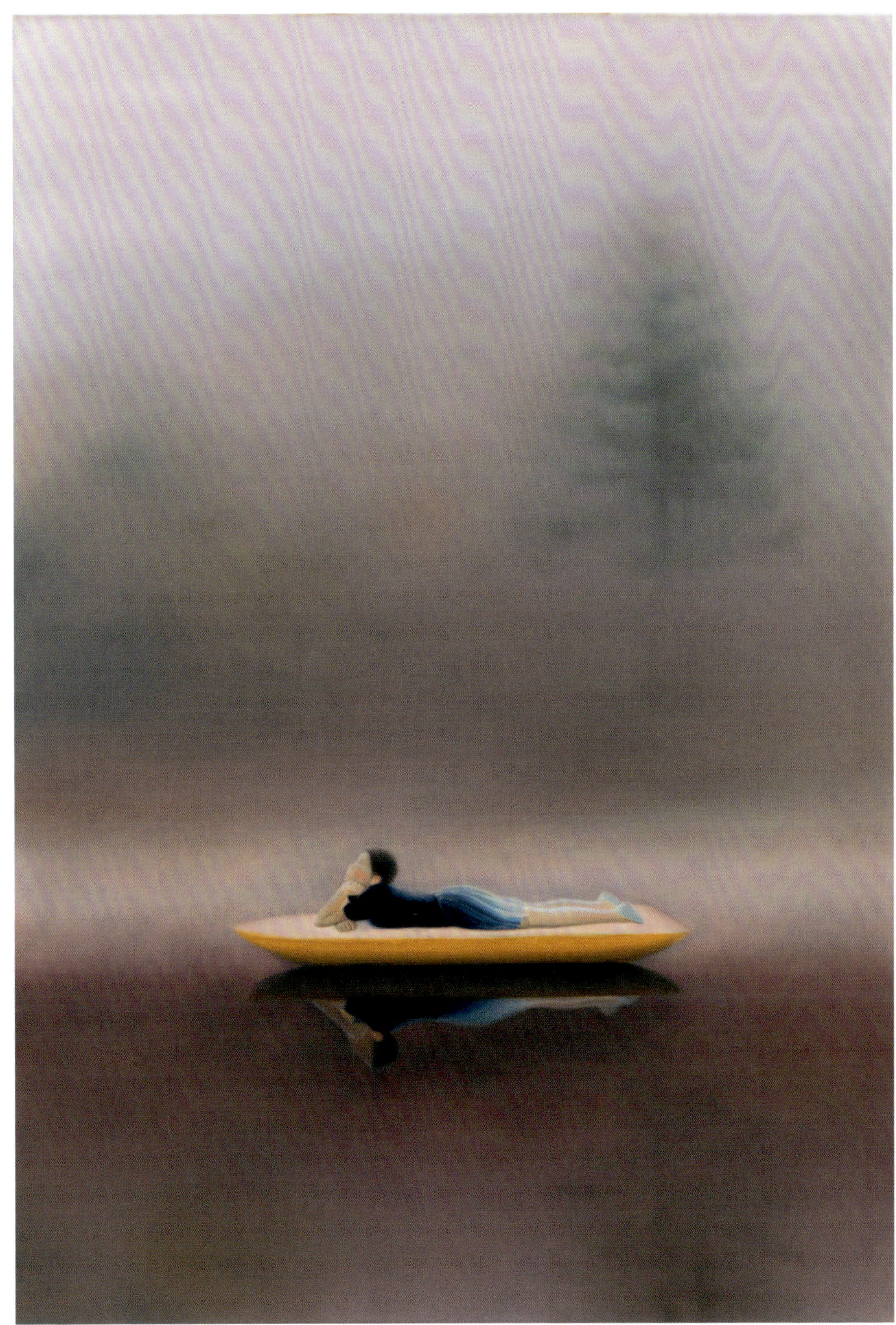

Sanbaishan 20, 2022
100 x 70 cm
Oil on canvas

Sanbaishan 30, 2023
160 x 120 cm
Oil on canvas

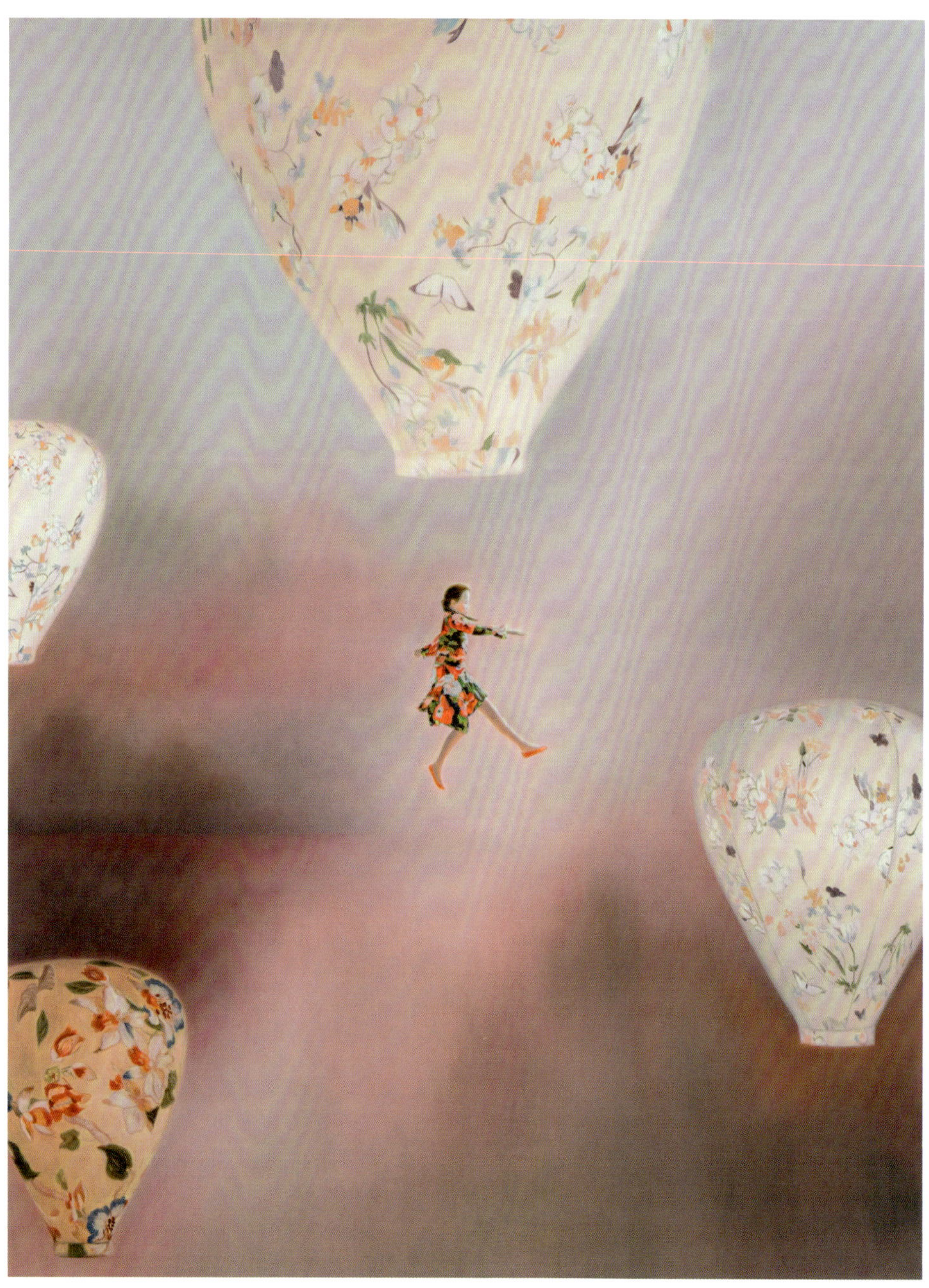

Sanbaishan 31, 2023
160 x 120 cm
Oil on canvas

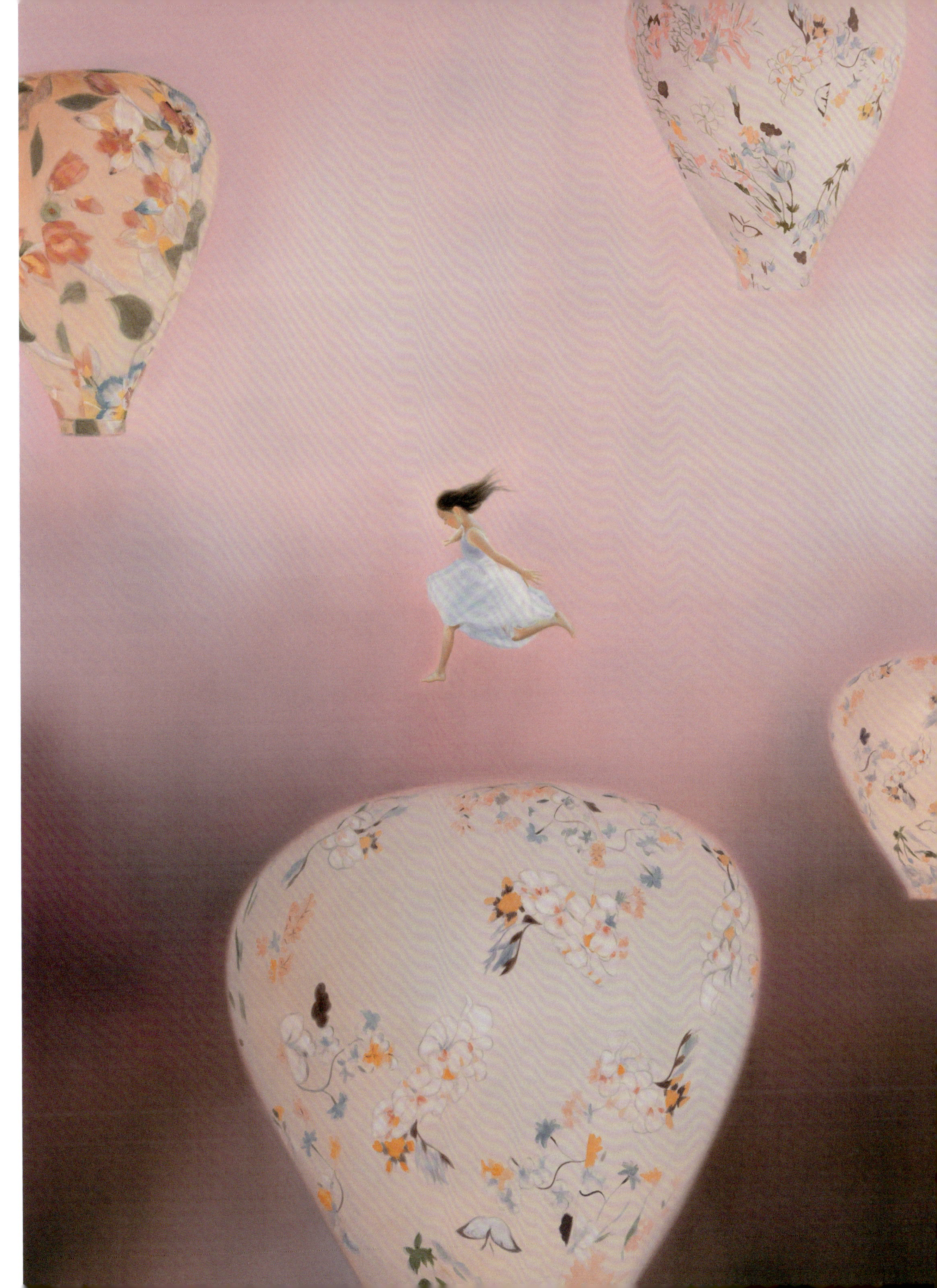

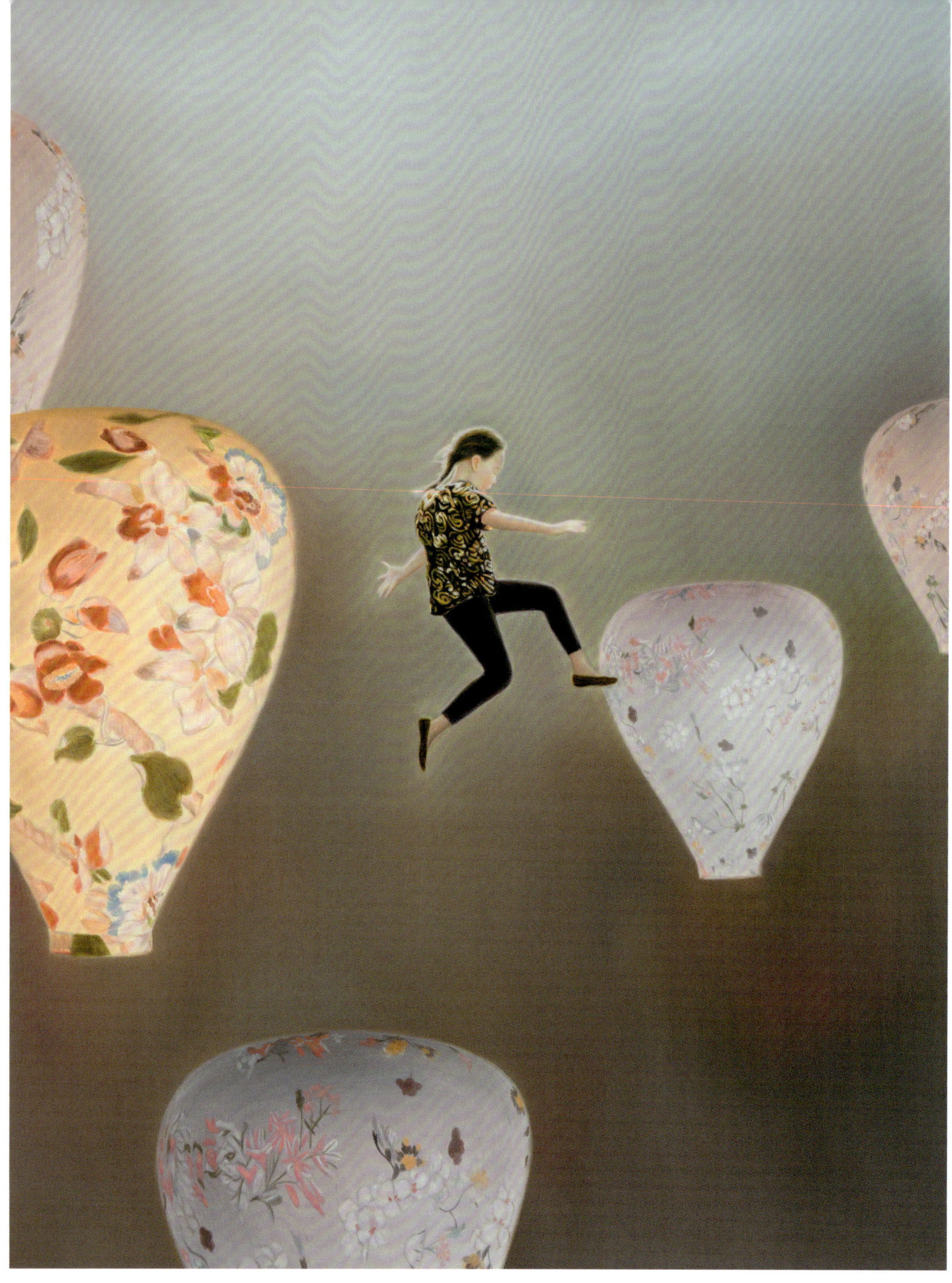

Sanbaishan 32, 2023
120 x 90 cm
Oil on canvas

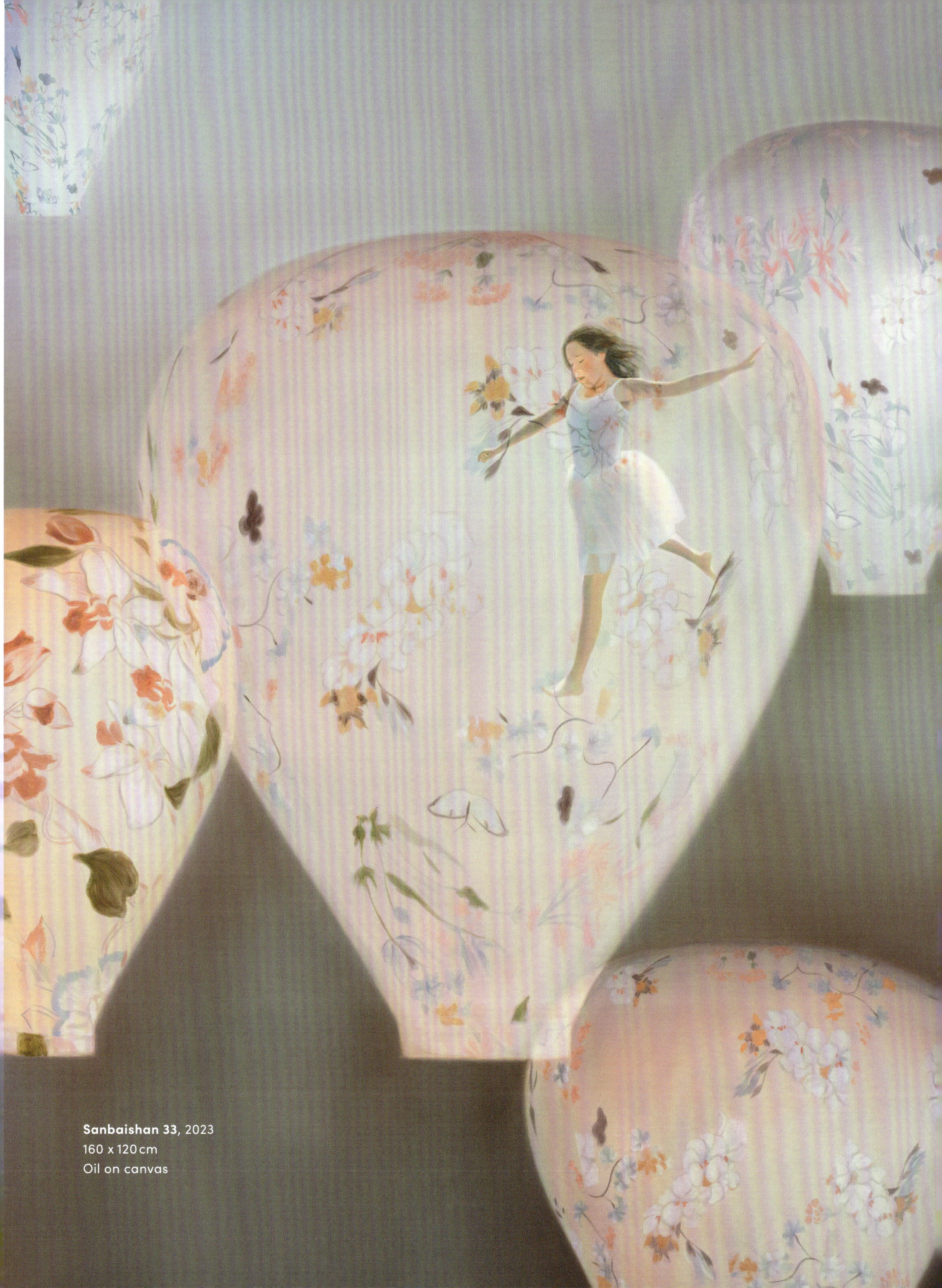

Sanbaishan 33, 2023
160 x 120 cm
Oil on canvas

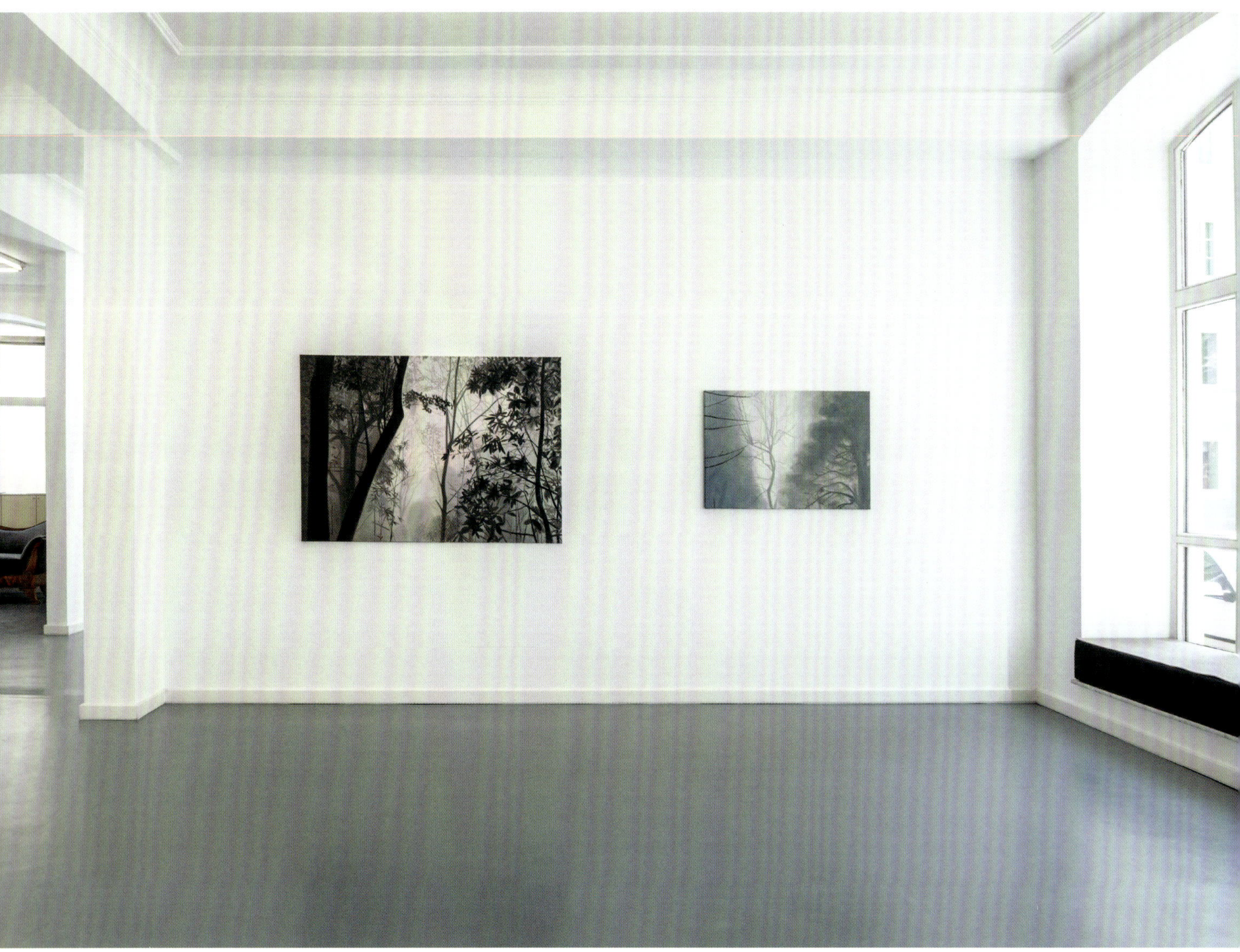

Solo Exhibition
Sanbaishan
Gallery Andreas Binder, 2018

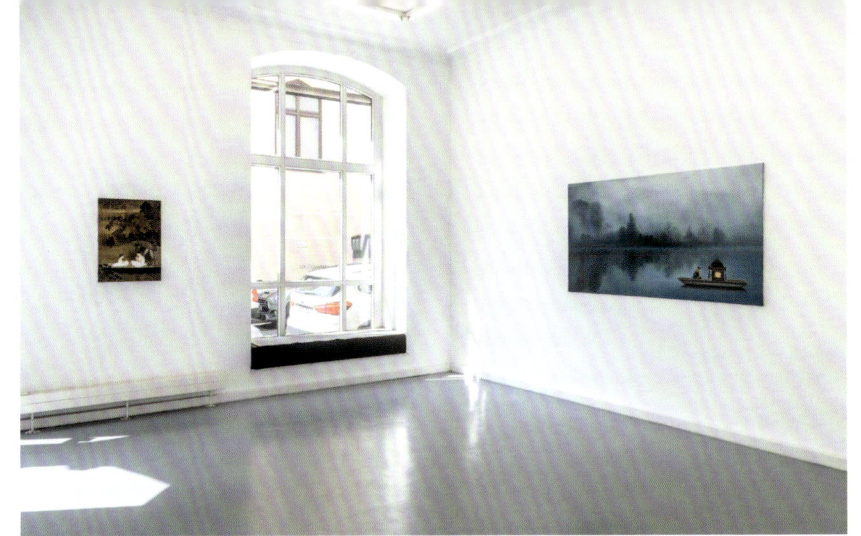

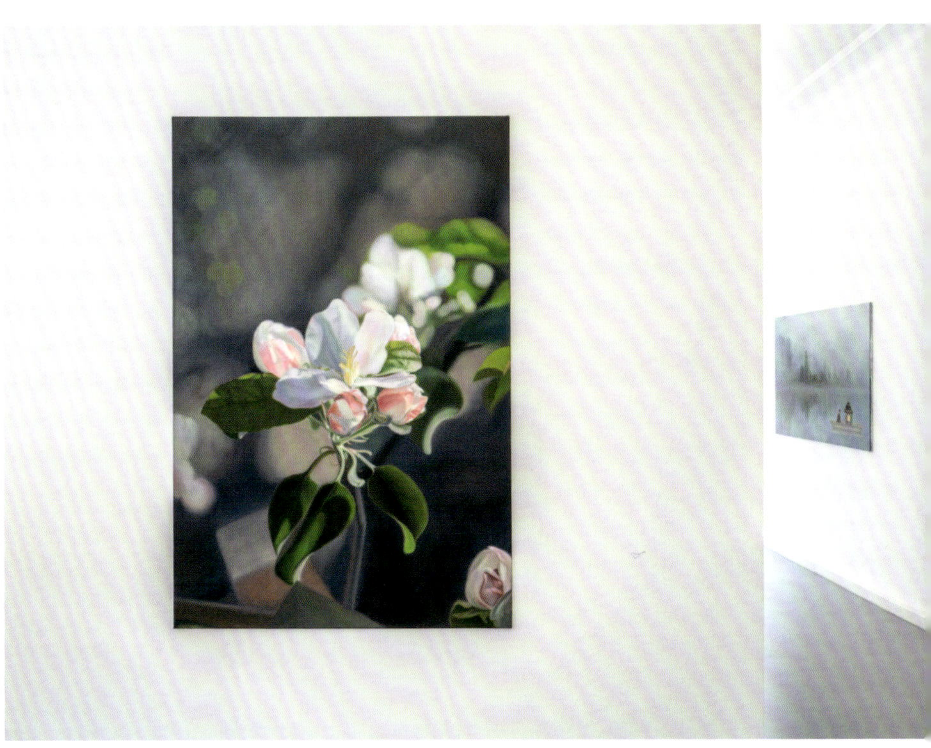

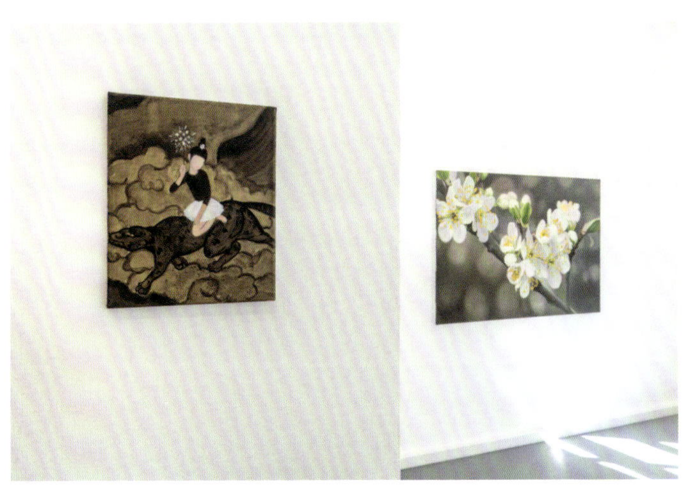

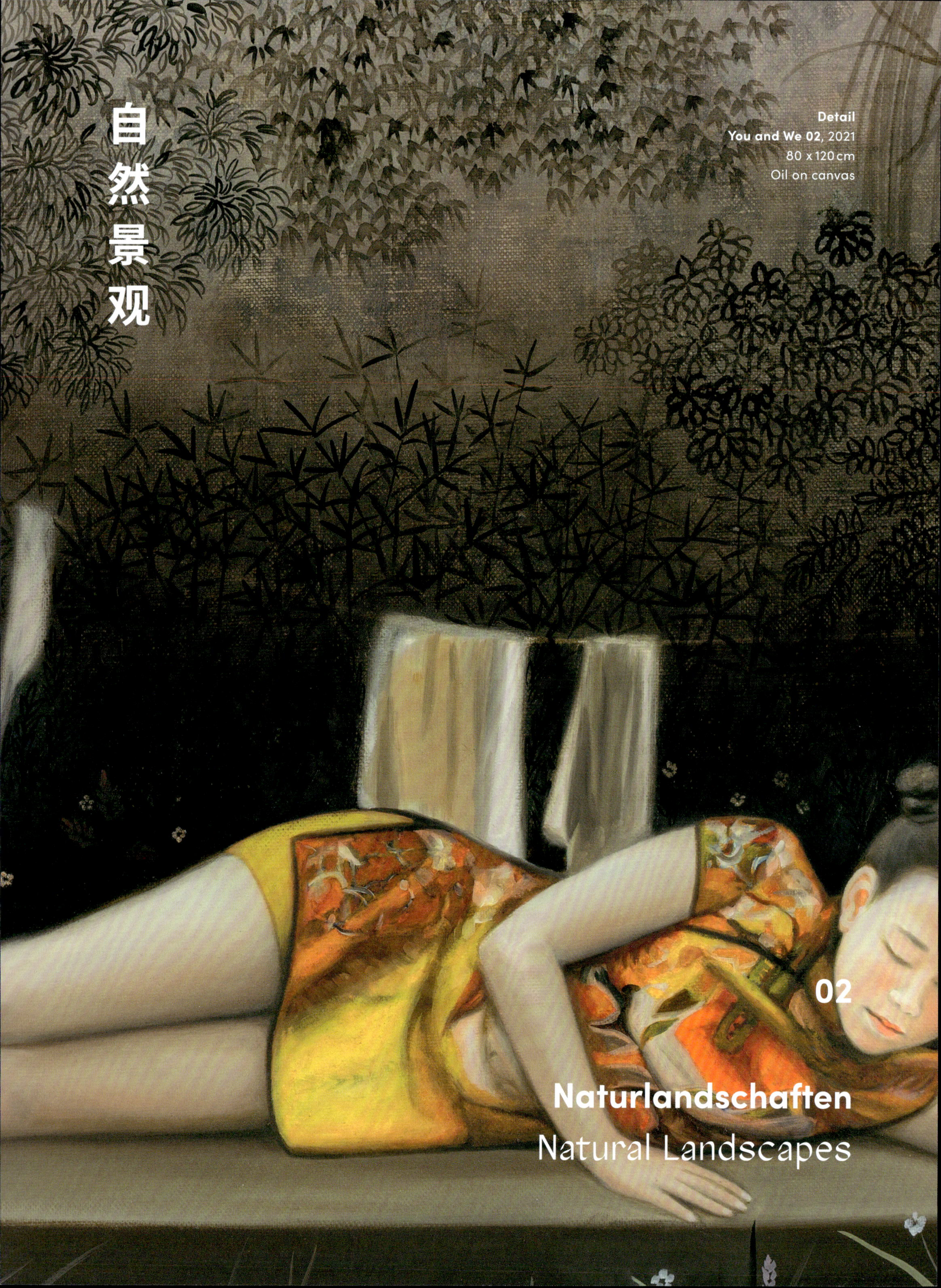
自然景观
Detail
You and We 02, 2021
80 x 120 cm
Oil on canvas
02
Naturlandschaften
Natural Landscapes

Im Kapitel Naturlandschaften hat Haiying Xu ihre künstlerischen Ideen konkret in Themen ausgedrückt. In Themen wie Schwester, Mutter und Kind, Mädchen mit Tiermotiven und Mädchen mit Booten. Die Künstlerin inszeniert die zwischenmenschlichen Beziehungen in einer natürlichen Umgebung. Die Natur als Gegensatz zur Kultur spielt seit Beginn von Haiying Xus künstlerischem Schaffen eine unverwechselbare Rolle. Ihre Nähe zur Natur beruht auf verschiedenen Gründen. Haiying Xu wuchs als Kind in einer natürlichen Umgebung in Jiangxi, China, auf. Erst als junge Erwachsene zog sie mit ihrer vierköpfigen Familie in die Metropole Shanghai. Nach einem sechsjährigen Studium der Malerei bei Professorin Anke Doberauer an der Akademie der Bildenden Künste in München lebte sie zehn Jahre als Familienmutter in ländlicher Umgebung bei Lübeck. Dort weckte die idyllische Lebensweise ihre Kindheitserinnerungen an die Natur. Obwohl die Naturerfahrungen aufgrund der unterschiedlichen klimatischen und geografischen Bedingungen in Jiangxi und Lübeck sehr verschieden waren und sich Vegetation, Wetter und Landschaft voneinander unterschieden. Dennoch verbindet sie ihre intensiven Naturerlebnisse an ihren persönlichen Aufenthaltsorten innerlich miteinander. Die Beziehung zwischen dort (Jiangxi-Heimat) und hier (Lübeck - Ort der Familiengründung) sowie zwischen der Vergangenheit in China und der Gegenwart in Deutschland bildet den Hintergrund für die ideelle Entwicklung der Künstlerin. Vor dieser Artikulation sind imaginäre Landschaften zu sehen, die Haiying Xu aus ihren verschiedenen Naturerfahrungen hybridisiert hat. Da dieser hybride Prozess unterschwellig in ihren künstlerischen Prozessen abläuft, gelingt es der Künstlerin, eine Authentizität zu erzeugen, in der die landschaftlichen Hintergründe in ihrer Malerei real erscheinen. In ihren Naturlandschaften wird ihre deutsch-romantische Sicht entfesselt, in der der Mensch nicht nur in einer konkreten realen Landschaft steht, sondern seine individuellen Empfindungen und Gedanken mit dieser scheinbaren Realität konfrontiert.

Vor diesem Hintergrund sind die Protagonisten in der Landschaftsmalerei von Haiying Xu zu sehen. Die weiblichen Figuren mit mädchenhaften Gesten, die mit ihrem Gegenüber zu interagieren scheinen, wirken entspannt und verträumt. Die in sich gekehrten Blicke der Mädchen zeigen dem Betrachter, dass sich die Mädchen ganz auf interaktive Situationen einlassen. Ob beim Flechten von Zöpfen, beim Spiel mit einem größeren Mädchen oder bei der Darstellung von Mutter und Kind, die Bilder machen die innige Beziehung der beiden Protagonisten sichtbar. So erlebt Haiying Xu ihre zwischenmenschlichen Beziehungen. Wie zu ihrer älteren Schwester, die die Künstlerin treu unterstützt, oder zu ihrem eigenen Sohn, der vor zehn Jahren in der ländlichen Umgebung von Lübeck geboren wurde. Ihre Liebe empfindet die chinesische Künstlerin als ebenso sanft und zärtlich wie Nebel und Wolken, die die Kanten der Berge entschärfen und die Naturlandschaften klimatisch harmonisieren. Die zwischenmenschlichen Momente strahlen Ruhe und Frieden aus. Der entdramatisierte Ausdruck der künstlerischen Sprache von Haiying Xu steht in einem Spannungsfeld zur europäischen Romantik, in der die Dramatik des aufgeklärten Individualismus im Vordergrund des künstlerischen Schaffens stand. Die künstlerische Sichtweise der chinesischen Künstlerin ist stark von der traditionellen chinesischen Malerei geprägt. Dort geht es in erster Linie darum, die Gefühle, Ideen und spirituellen Vorstellungen des Künstlers auszudrücken und nicht darum, die Landschaften naturgetreu wiederzugeben. Es ist ein Versuch, den Gemütszustand des Künstlers mit der Stimmung der Naturlandschaft, die er in dieser hervorruft, in Einklang zu bringen. Die Interaktion zwischen den dargestellten Protagonisten, die der Künstler in der Naturlandschaft malerisch schildert, kann als Übersetzung der inneren Befindlichkeit des Künstlers in scheinbar banale menschliche Handlungen verstanden werden. Die Ausdrucksweise des scheinbar Banalen ist das Mittel, mit dem der Künstler eine entdramatisierte Wirkung erzielt und für die Kunst einen Zugang zum Leben schafft.

Die verschiedenen Sichtweisen aus chinesischen und deutschen Kulturkreisen auf die Beziehung zwischen der Natur und dem Menschen hat Haiying Xu in ihrer Malerei erfahrbar hervorgebracht.

In the chapter "Natural landscapes" Haiying Xu expressed her artistic ideas in specific themes, like sister, mother and child, girl with animal motifs and girl with boats. The artist stages the interpersonal relationships in natural surroundings. Since the beginning of Haiying Xu's artistic career, the depiction of nature as a contrast to culture has always played an unmistakeable role. There are various reasons for her closeness to nature. As a child, Haiying Xu grew up in a natural environment in Jiangxi, China. It was only as a young adult that she moved to the metropolis of Shanghai with her family of four. After studying painting for six years under Professor Anke Doberauer at the Akademie der Bildenden Künste (Academy of Fine Arts) in Munich, she spent ten years looking after her children in a rural area near Lübeck. There, the idyllic way of life reawakened her childhood memories of nature, even though the experiences of nature in Jiangxi and Lübeck were very different due to the distinct climatic and geographical conditions and the disparities in vegetation, weather and landscape. Nonetheless, she inwardly connected her intense experiences of nature with her personal whereabouts. The relationship between there (Jiangxi – her homeland) and here (Lübeck – where she started a family) as well as between the past in China and the present in Germany forms the background for the ideational evolution of the artist. With this in mind, you can see imaginary landscapes, which Haiying Xu hybridized, combining her various experiences of nature. Since this hybrid process subliminally runs through her artistic processes, the artist is able to create an authenticity, in which the landscapes used as backgrounds in her paintings appear to be real. In her natural landscapes, her romantic German perspective is unleashed, in which the human being is not only pictured in a specific real landscape, but his/her individual emotions and thoughts are confronted with this supposed reality.

In front of this backdrop, you can see the protagonists in Haiying Xu's landscape painting. The female figures, who seem interact with their counterparts with girlish gestures, appear relaxed and dreamy. The girls' introspective looks show the observer that the girls are fully engaged in interactive situations. Whether the pictures depict girls plaiting pigtails, games with an older girl or the portrayal of a mother and child, the pictures make the intimate relationship between the two protagonists visible. That is how Haiying Xu experiences her interpersonal relationships. Like her relationship with her older sister, who loyally supports the artist, or with her own son, who was born ten years ago in the rural surroundings of Lübeck. The Chinese artist perceives her love as being as soft and tender as mist and clouds, which soften the sharp edges of the mountains and climatically harmonize natural landscapes. The interpersonal moments emit a sense of peace and quiet. The de-dramatized expression of Haiying Xu's artistic language remains in conflict with European Romanticism, in which the drama of enlightened individualism is at the forefront of artistic work. The artistic perspective of the Chinese artist is strongly influenced by traditional Chinese painting. Here, it is primarily about feelings, ideas and the expression of the artist's spiritual notions, rather than being about the realistic depiction of landscapes. It is an attempt to bring the artist's frame of mind into harmony with the atmosphere of the natural landscape that the artist evokes it in. The interaction between the represented protagonists, which the artist's paintings portray in natural landscapes, can be understood as a translation of the inner sensitivities of the artist in seemingly banal, human situations. This way of expressing the apparently banal is the means with which the artist achieves a de-dramatized effect and makes art seem relatable to real life.

In her paintings Haiying Xu tangibly highlights the various perspectives taken from Chinese and German cultural milieux with regards to the relationship between nature and human beings. Chinese and German cultures on the relationship between nature and humans in her painting.

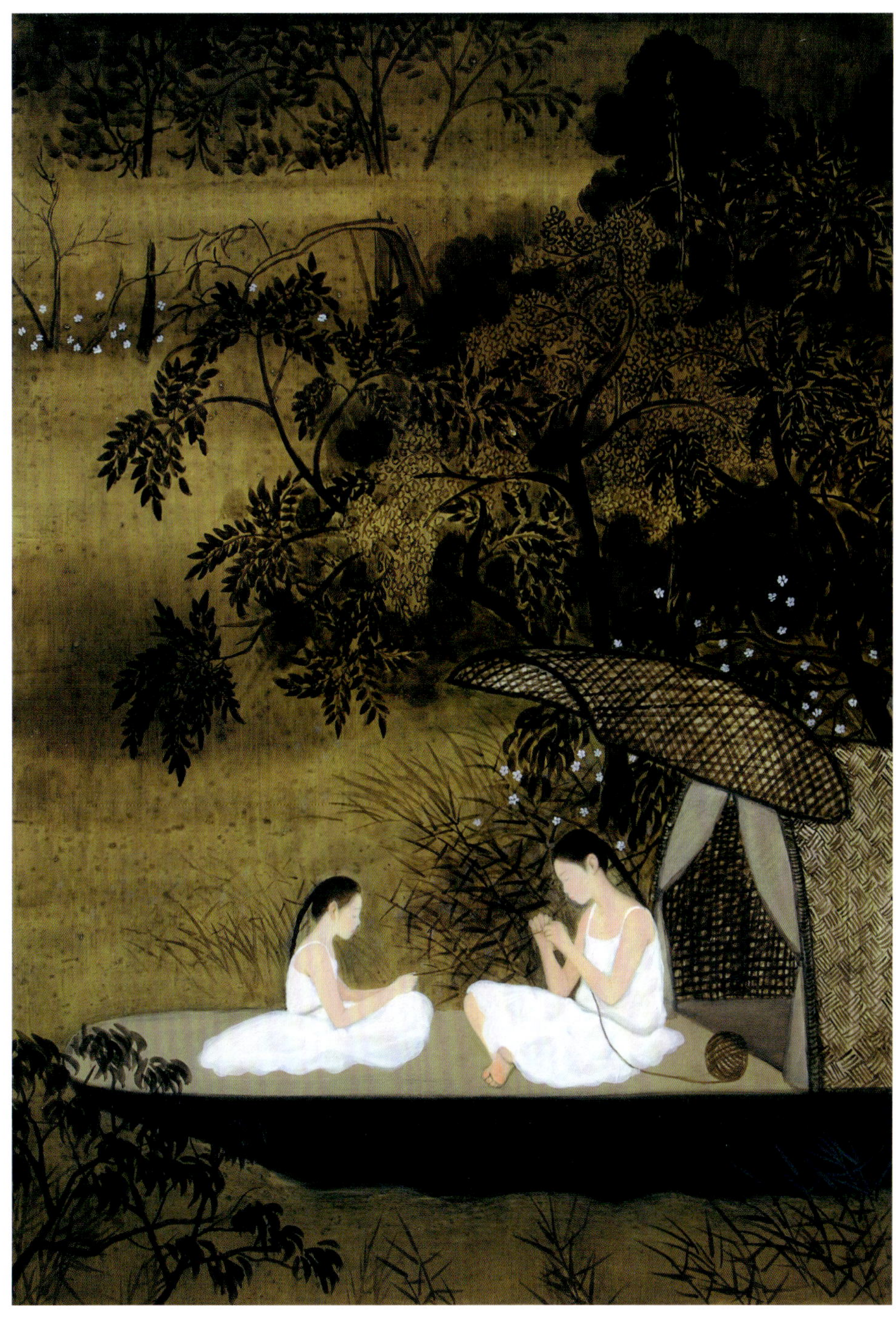

Girls with Boat 012, 2017
70 x 50 cm
Oil on wood

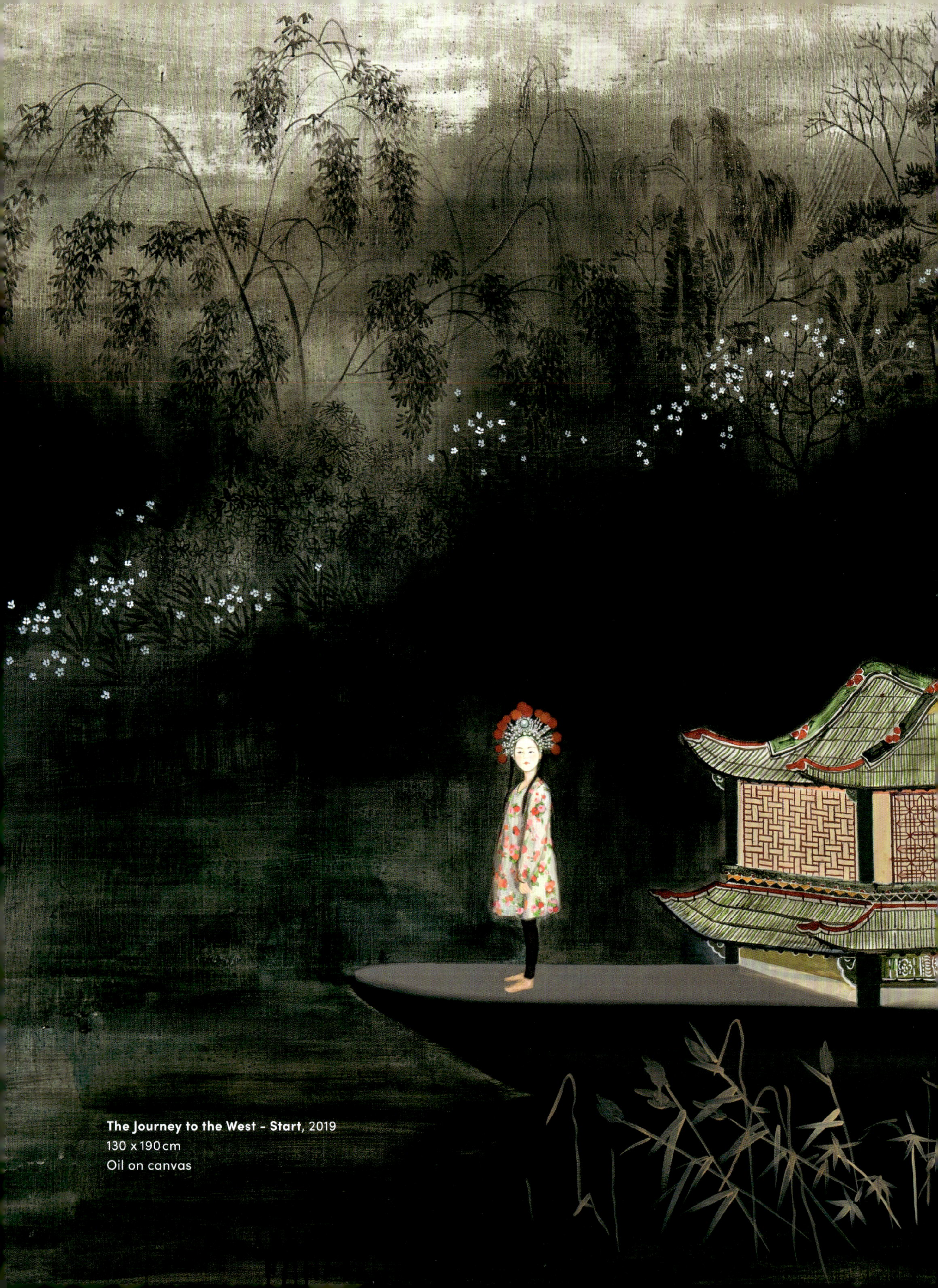

The Journey to the West – Start, 2019
130 x 190 cm
Oil on canvas

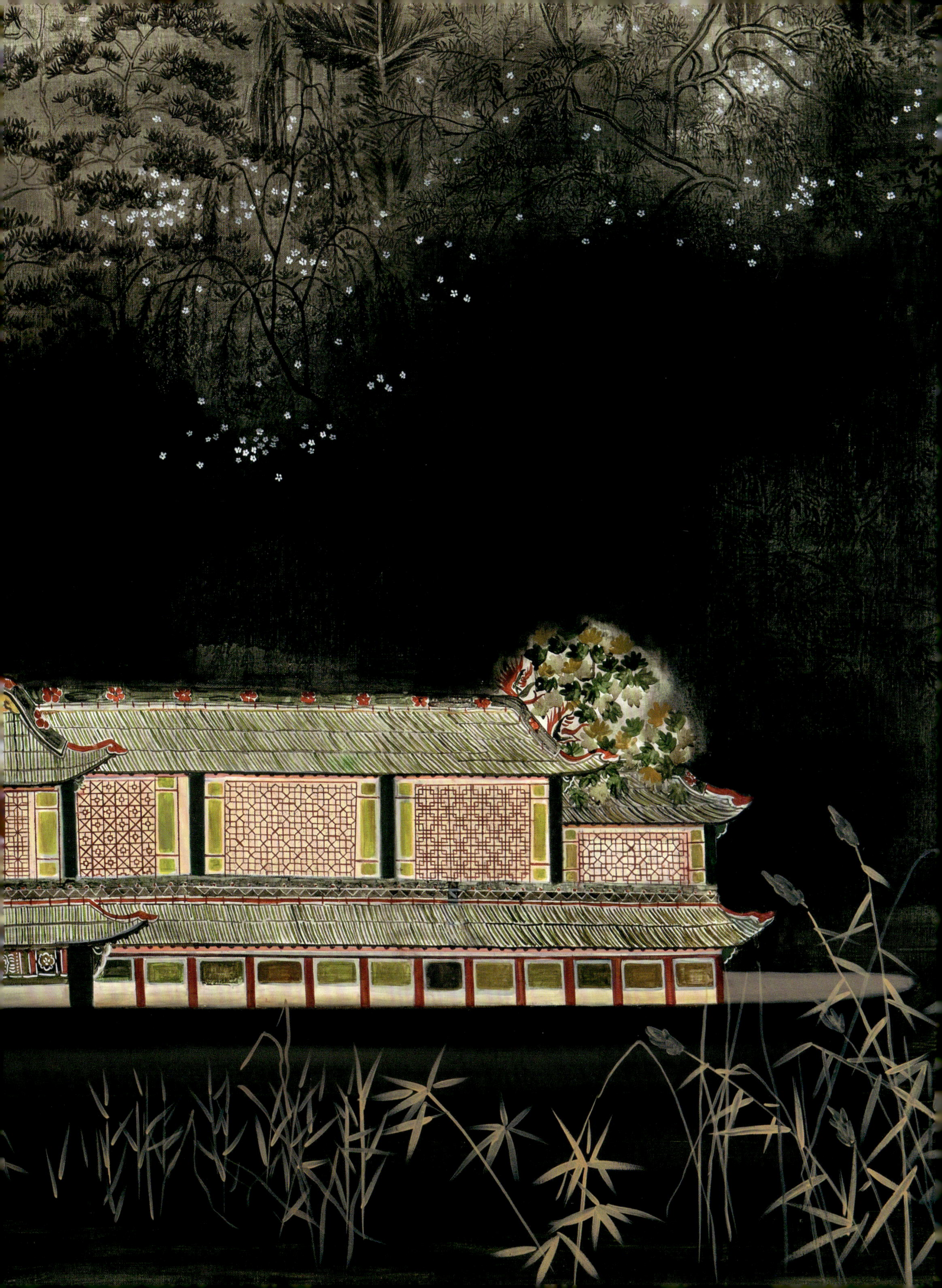

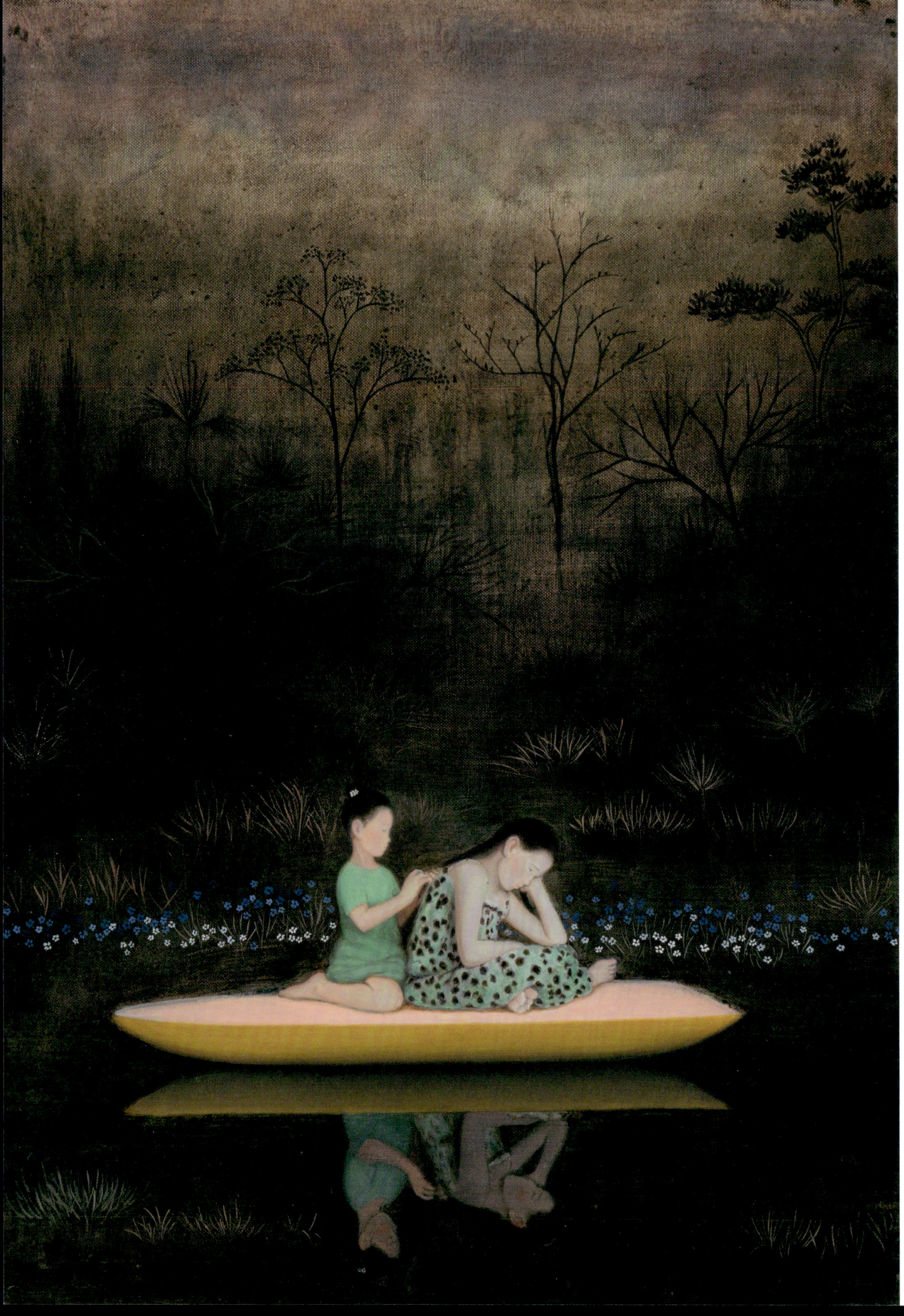

You and We 03, 2018
100 x 70 cm
Oil on canvas

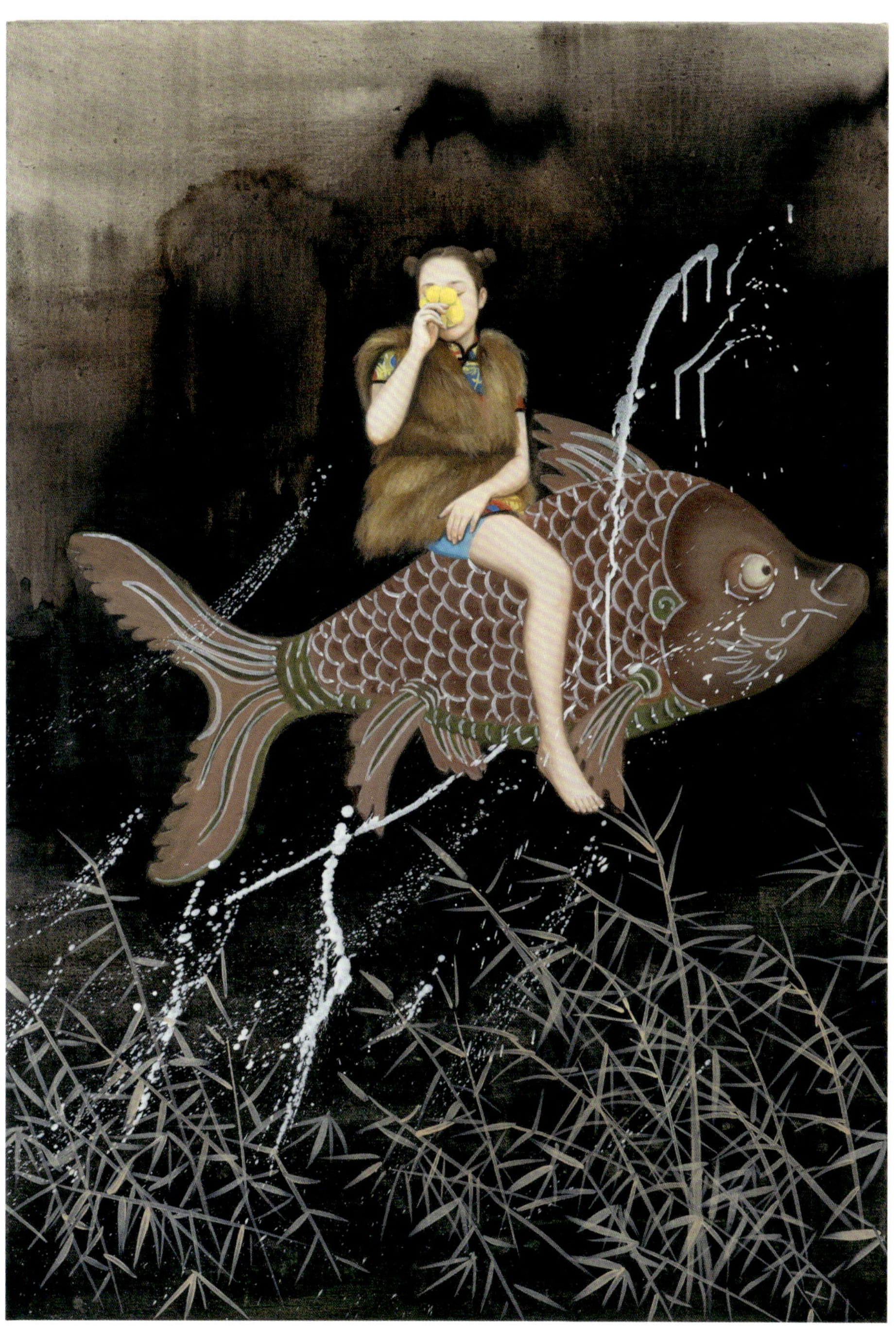

The Sister 02, 2022
70 x 50 cm
Oil on canvas

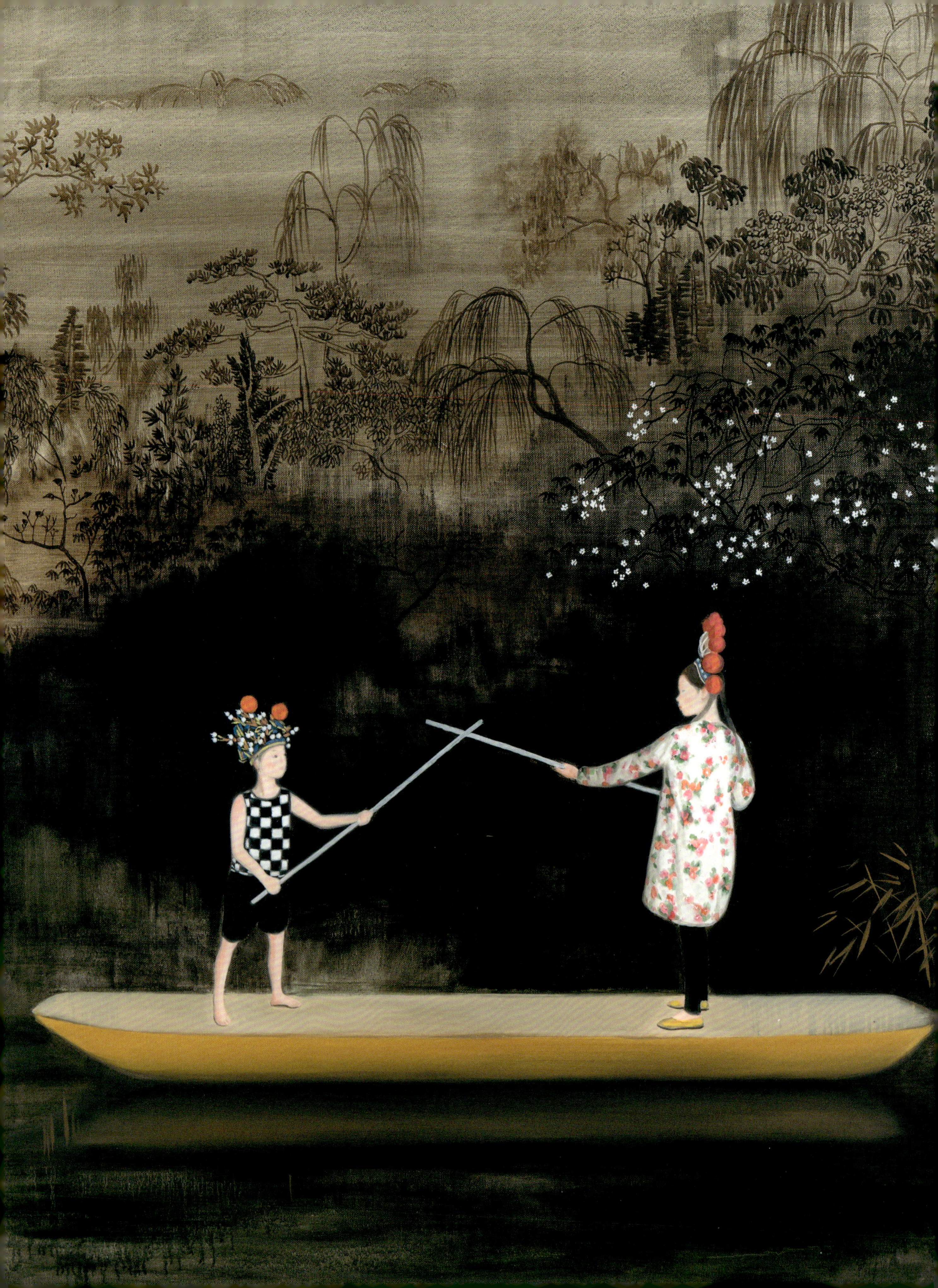

Girls with Boat 009, 2017
70 x 50 cm
Oil on wood

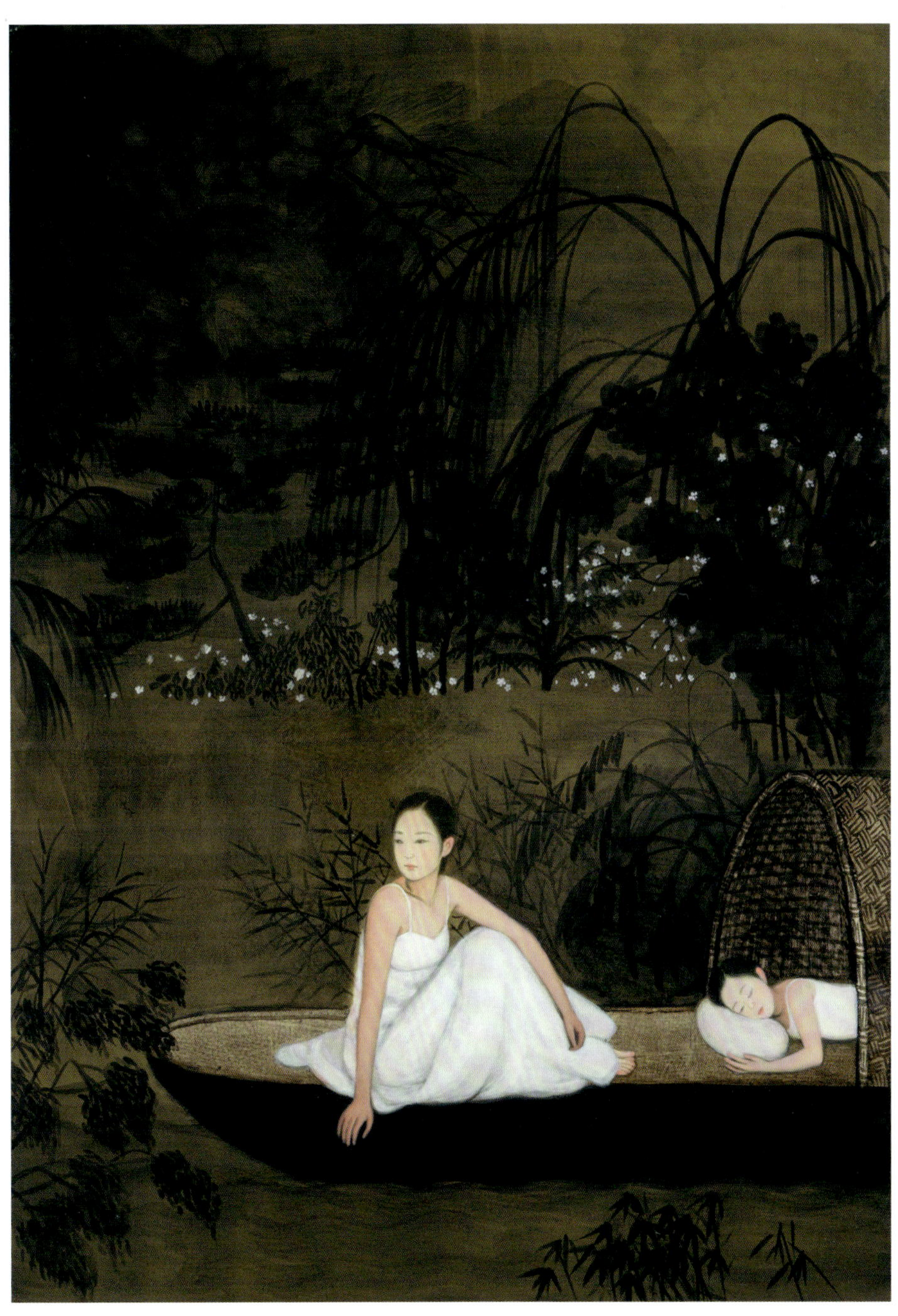

You and We, 2018
125 x 100 cm
Oil on canvas

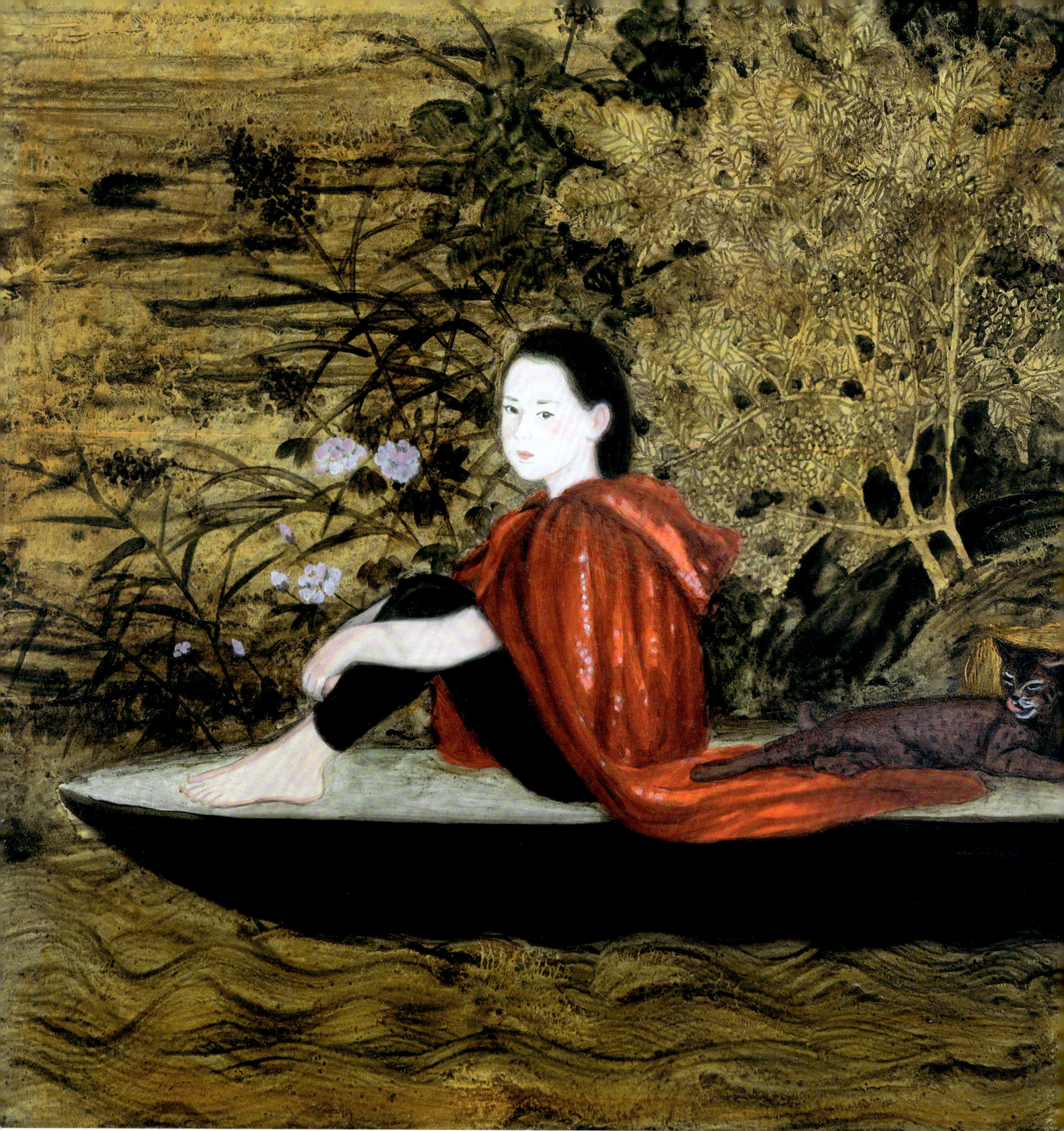

Girl with Boat and Cat, 2022
30 x 30 cm
Oil on wood

Girl with Boat 011, 2022
30 x 30 cm
Oil on wood

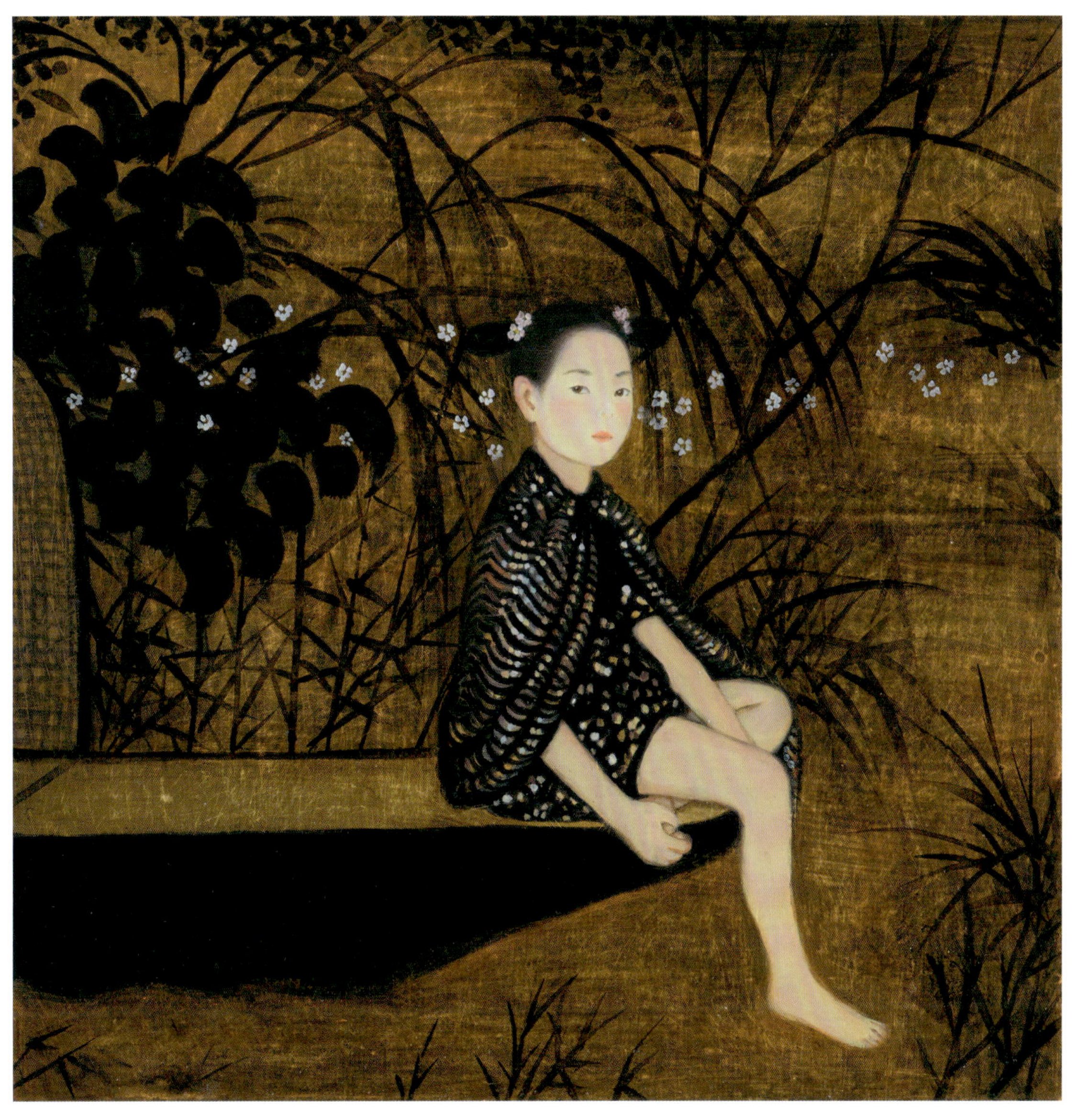

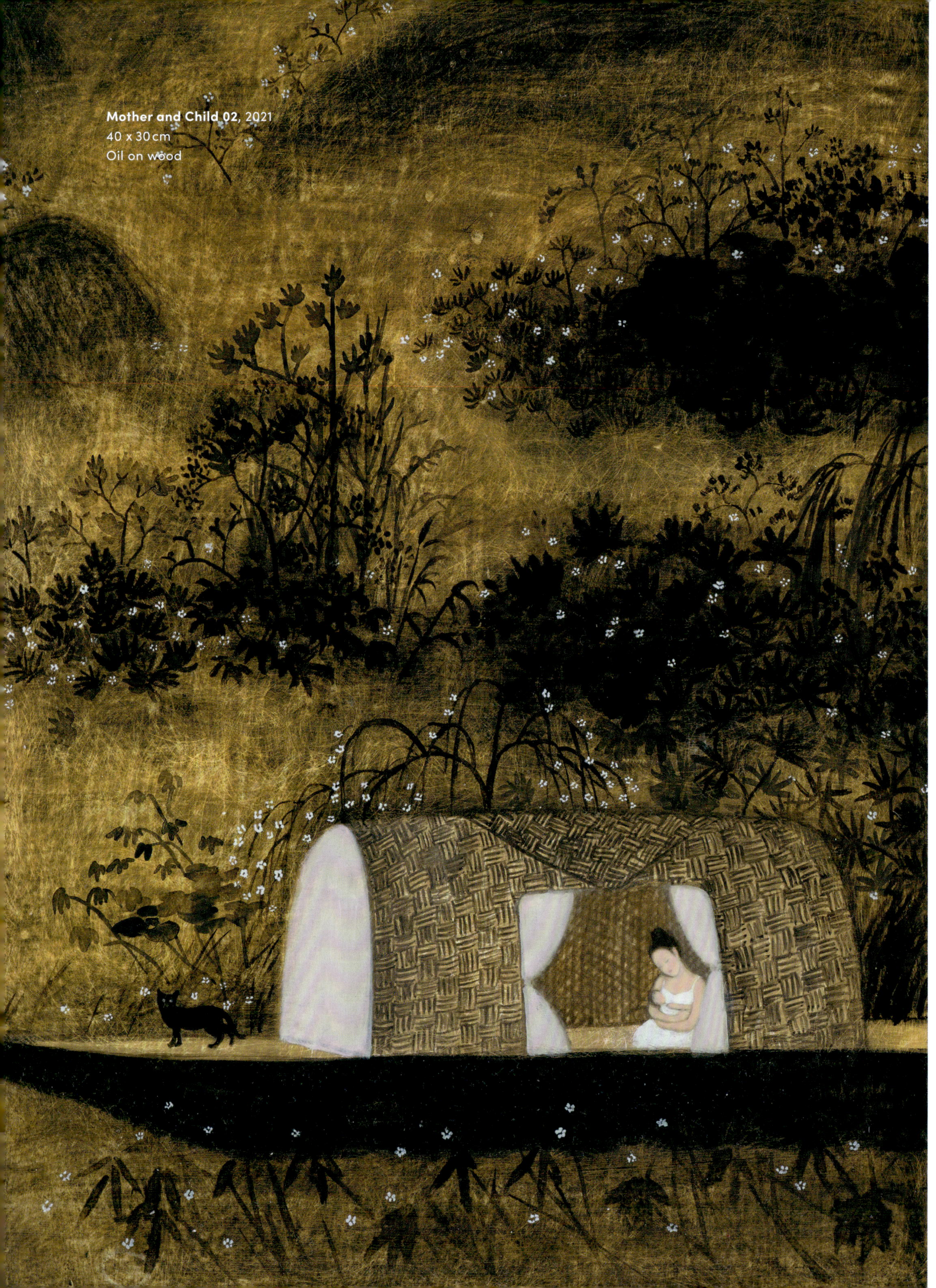

Mother and Child 02, 2021
40 x 30 cm
Oil on wood

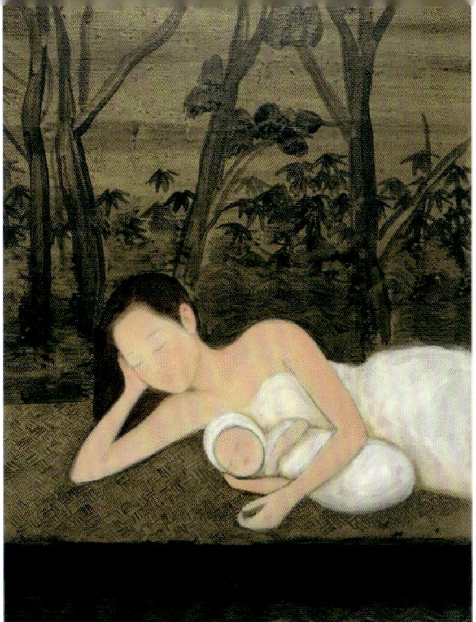

The little Sea 002, 2017
30 x 24 cm
Oil on canvas

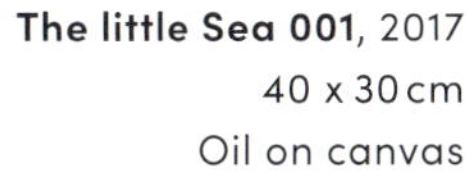

The little Sea 001, 2017
40 x 30 cm
Oil on canvas

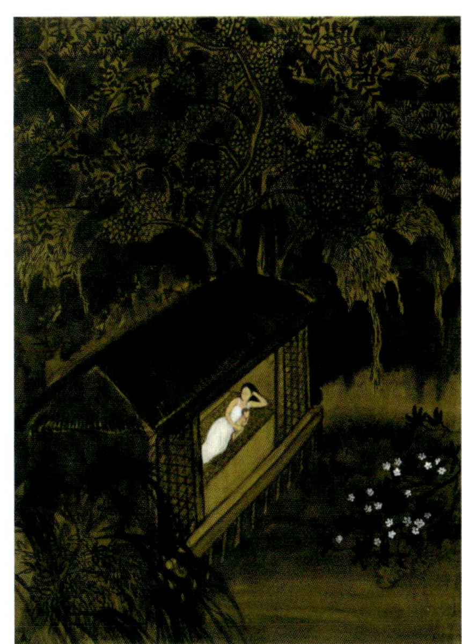

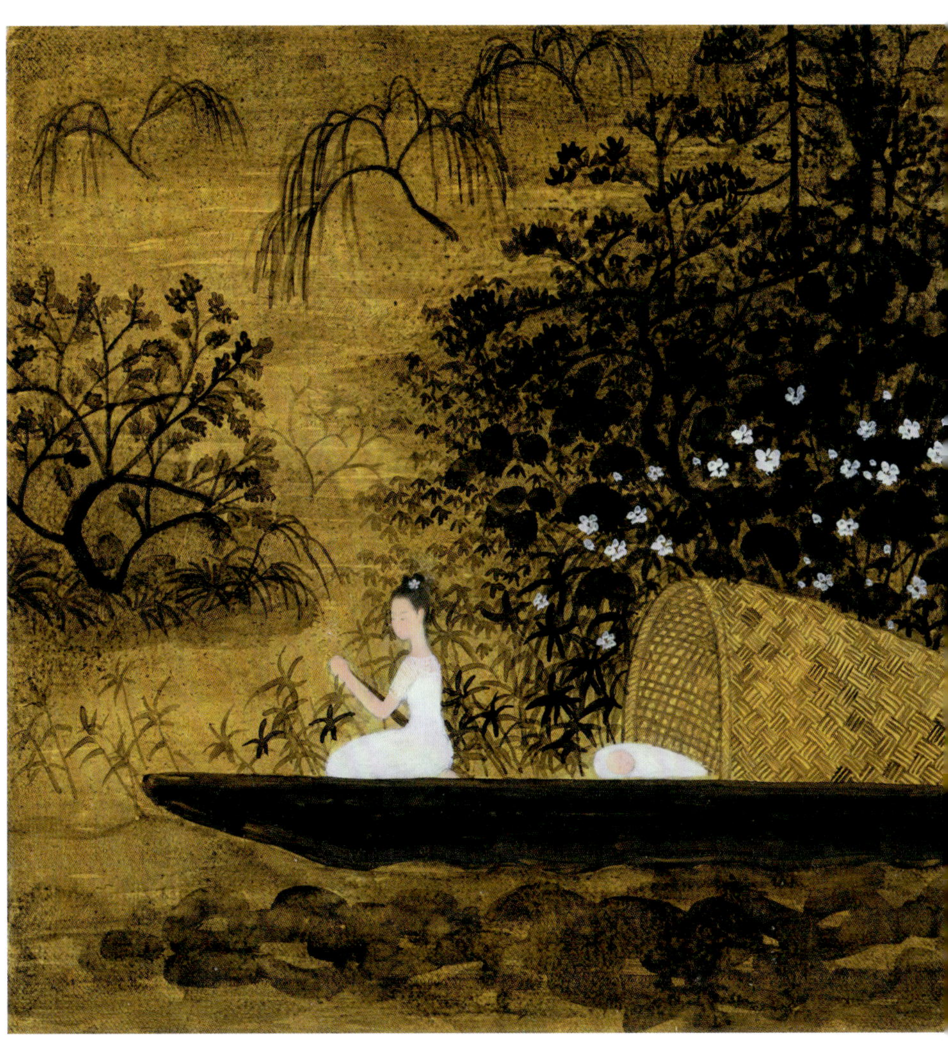

Mother and Child 01, 2017
30 x 30 cm
Oil on canvas

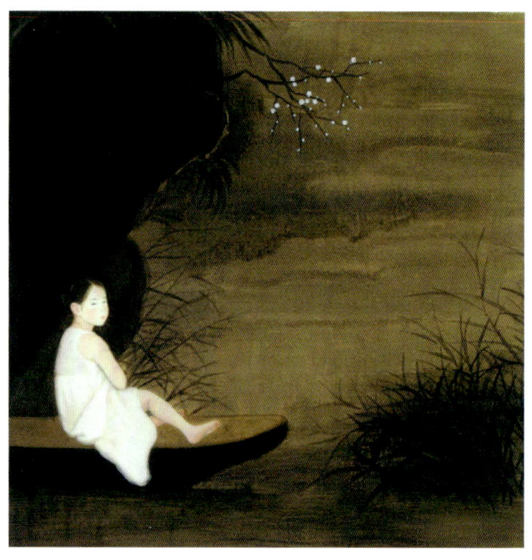

Girl with Boat 005, 2017
30 x 20 cm
Oil on canvas

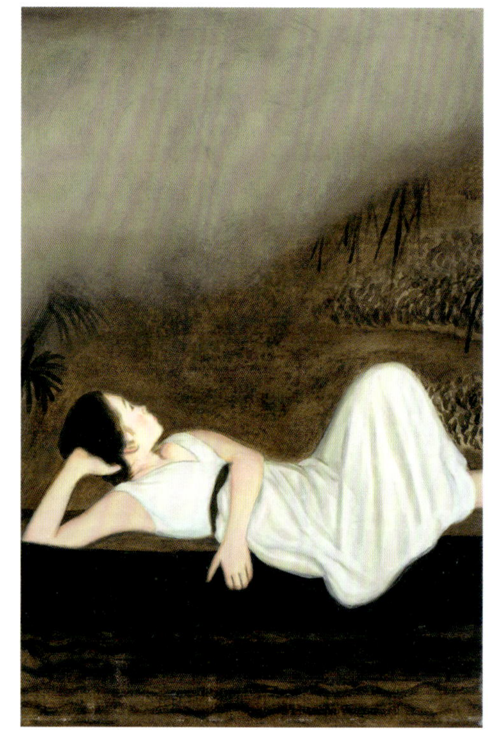

Girl with Boat 008, 2017
50 x 50 cm
Oil on canvas

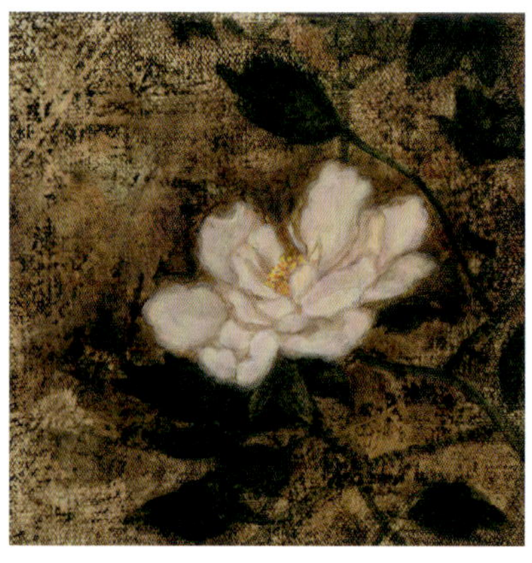

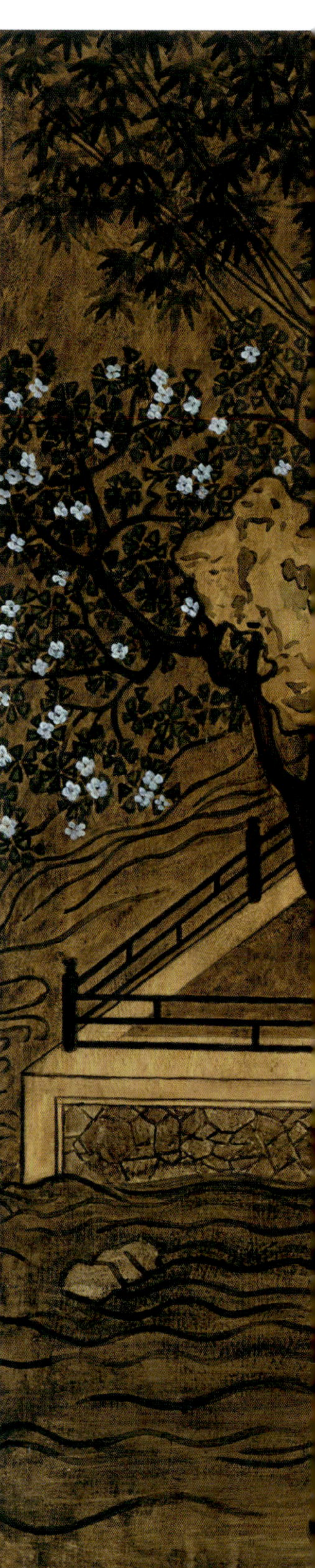

Peony, 2022
20 x 20 cm
Oil on canvas

Niu Niu, 2020
80 x 100 cm
Oil on wood

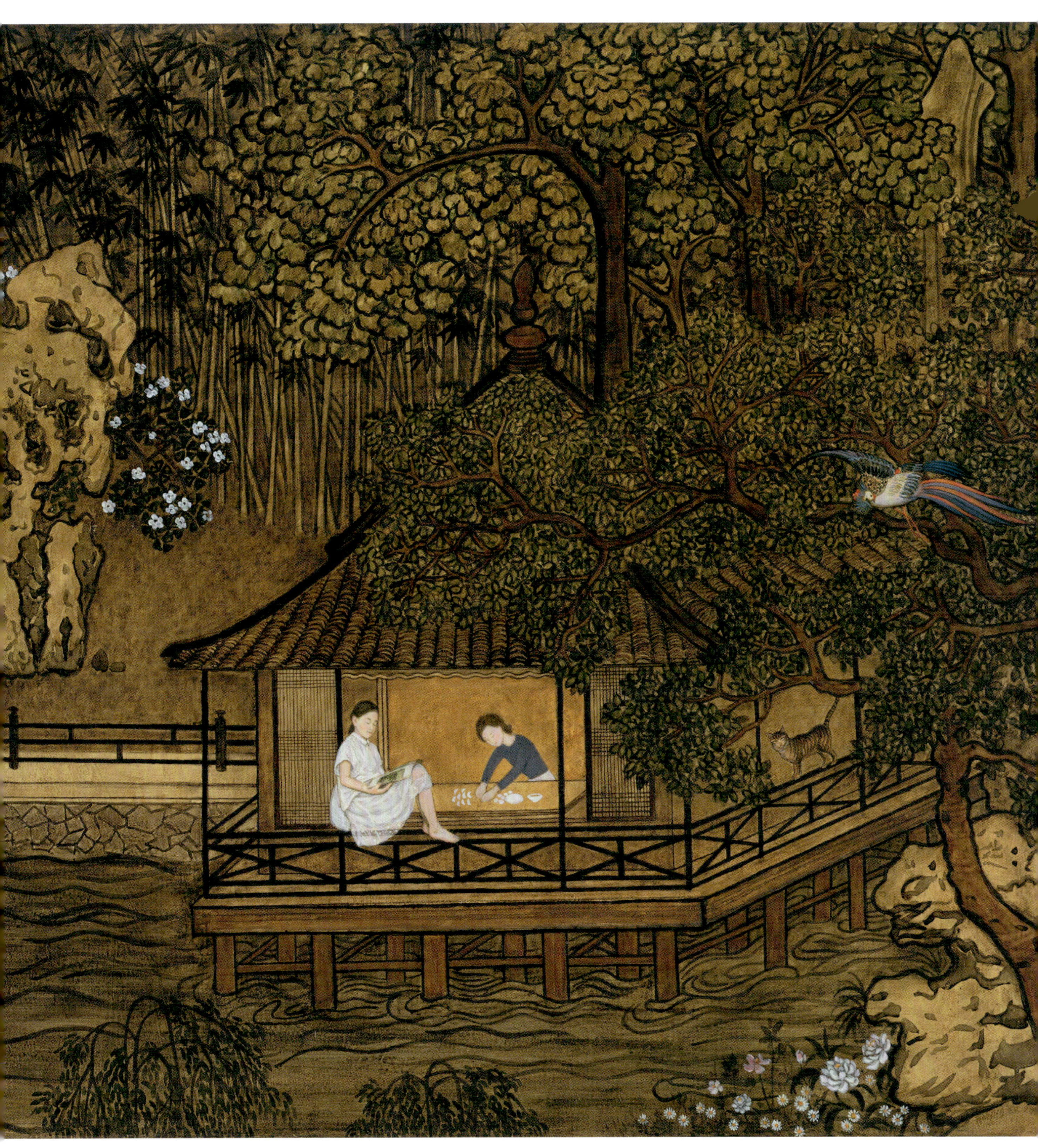

Girl with Boat 007, 2017
60 x 60 cm
Oil on wood

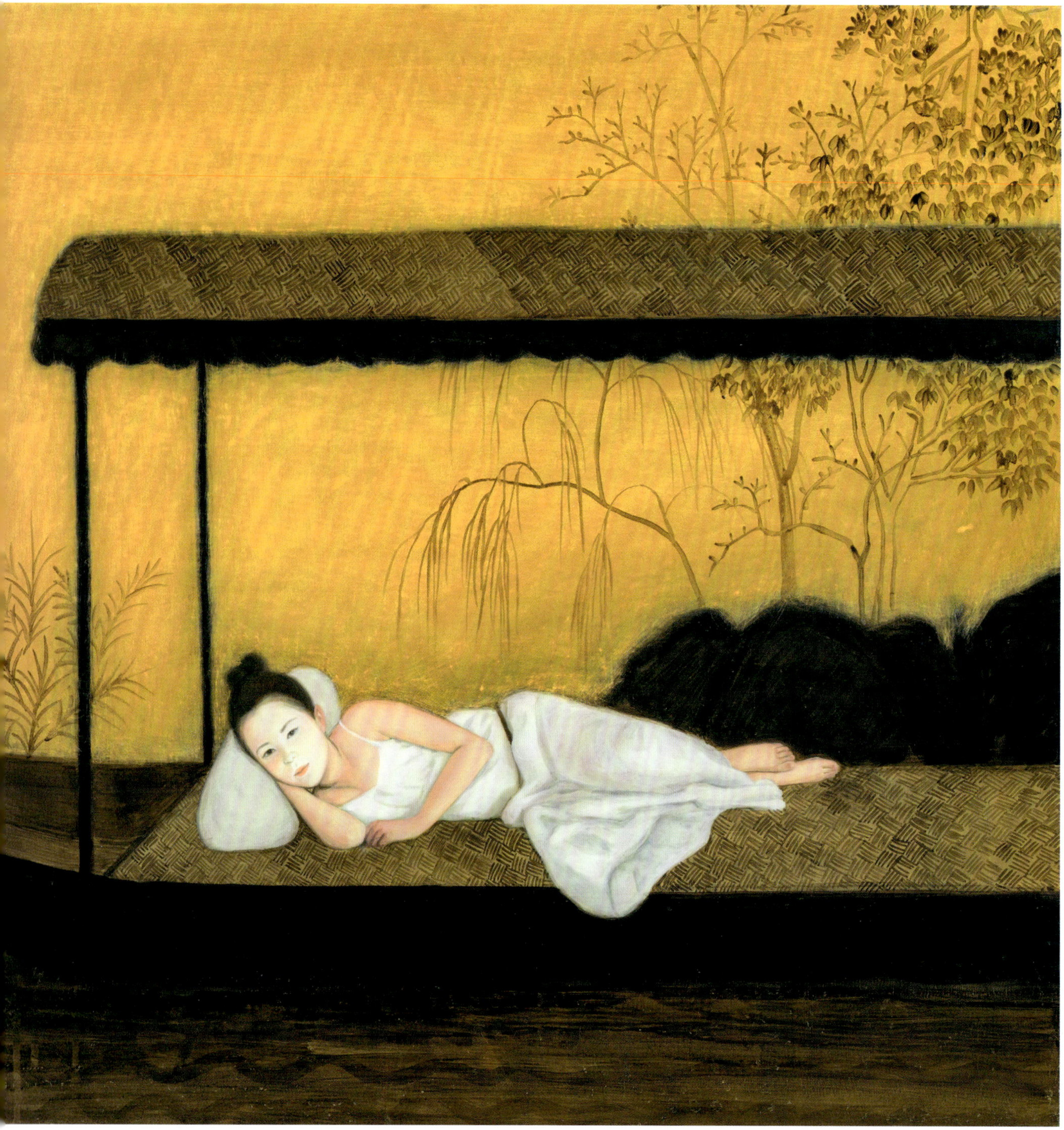

Girl with Boat 002, 2017
30 x 30 cm
Oil on canvas

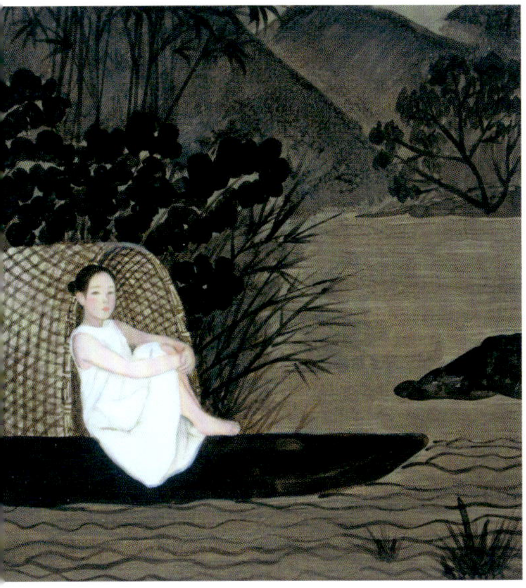

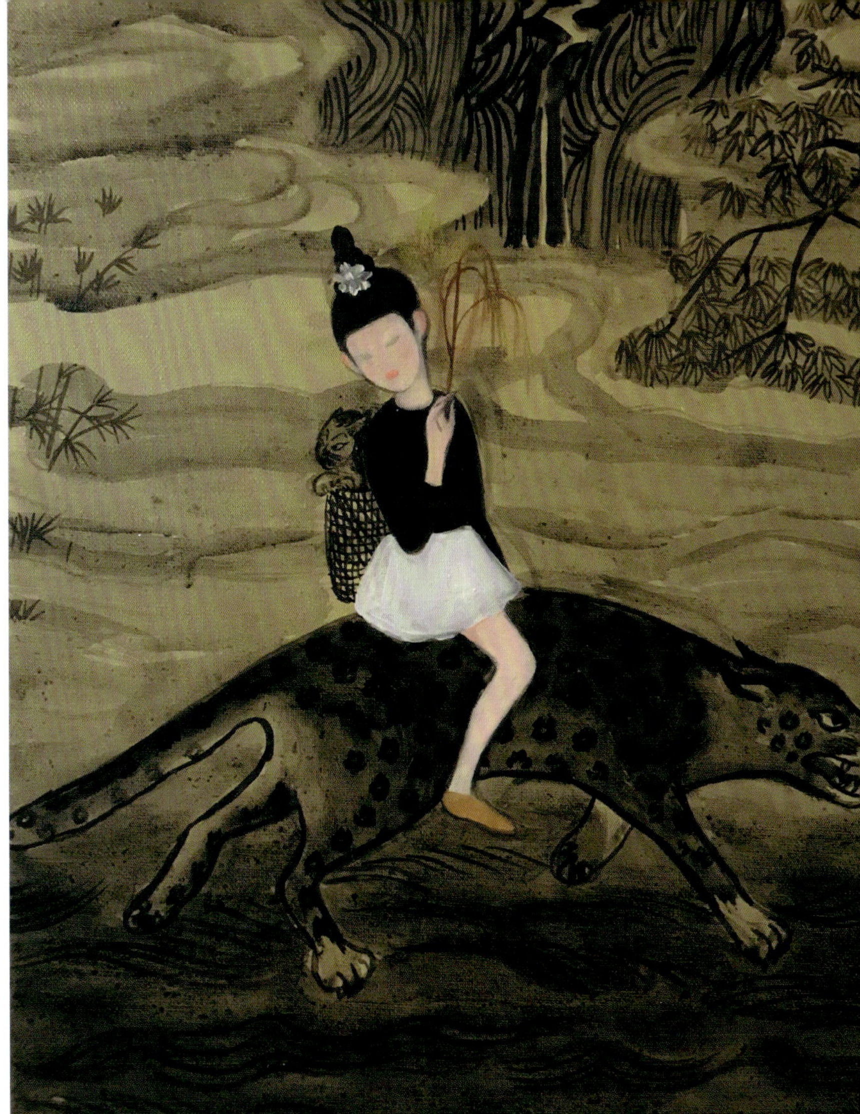

Girl with Tiger 001, 2017
30 x 24 cm
Oil on canvas

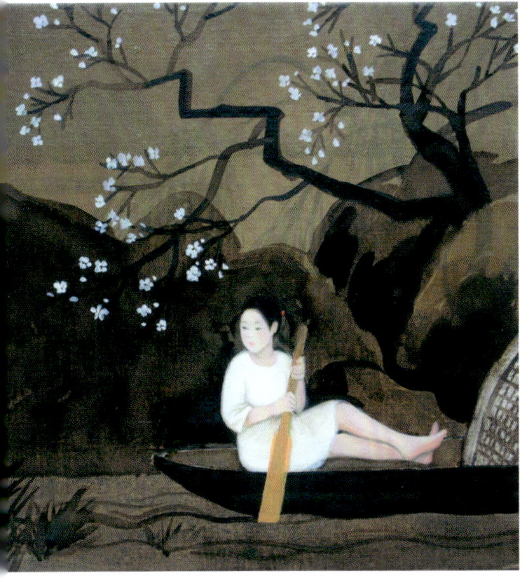

Girl with Boat 001, 2017
30 x 30 cm
Oil on canvas

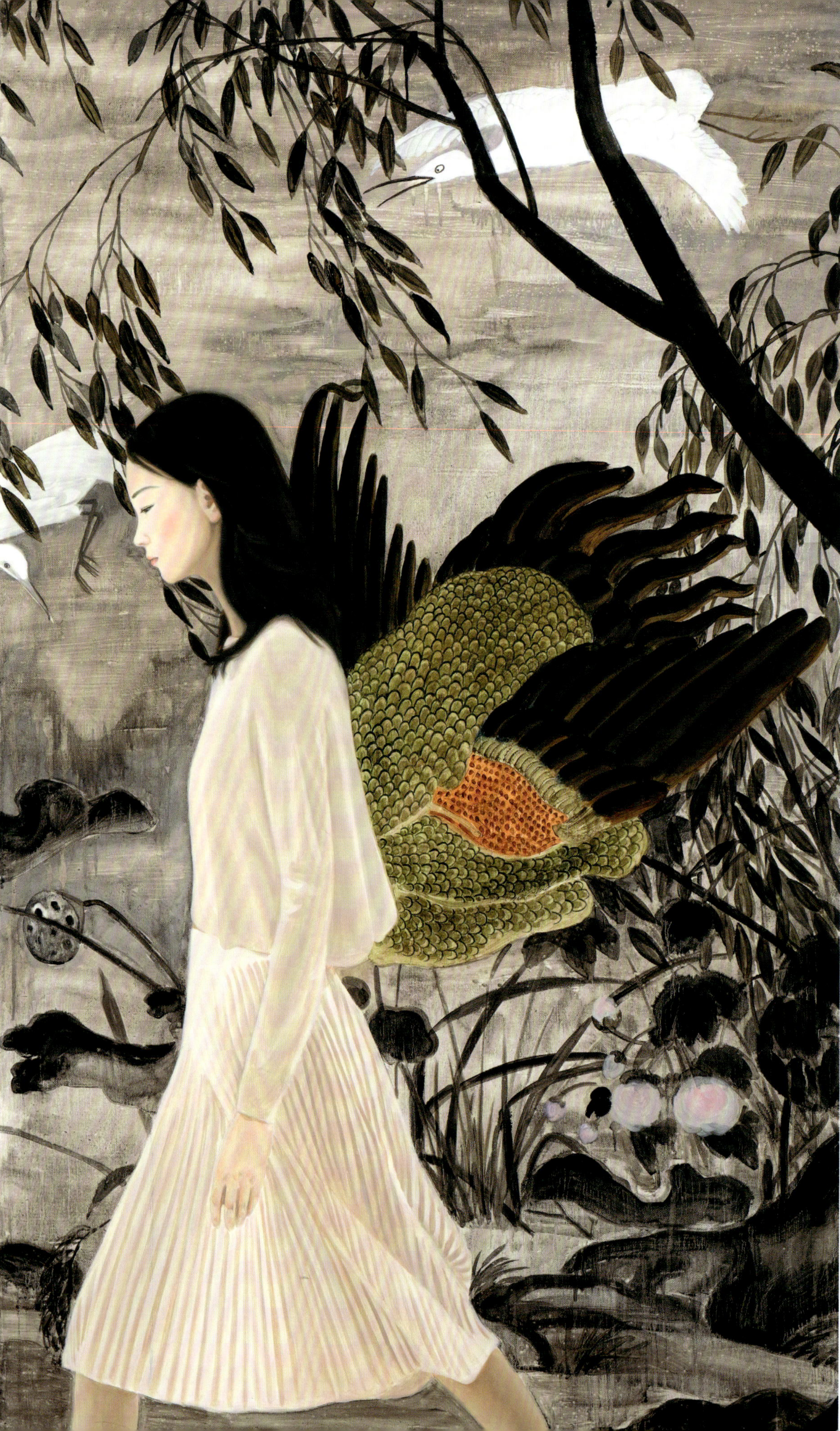

Sea Eagle 13, 2019
150 x 90 cm
Oil on canvas

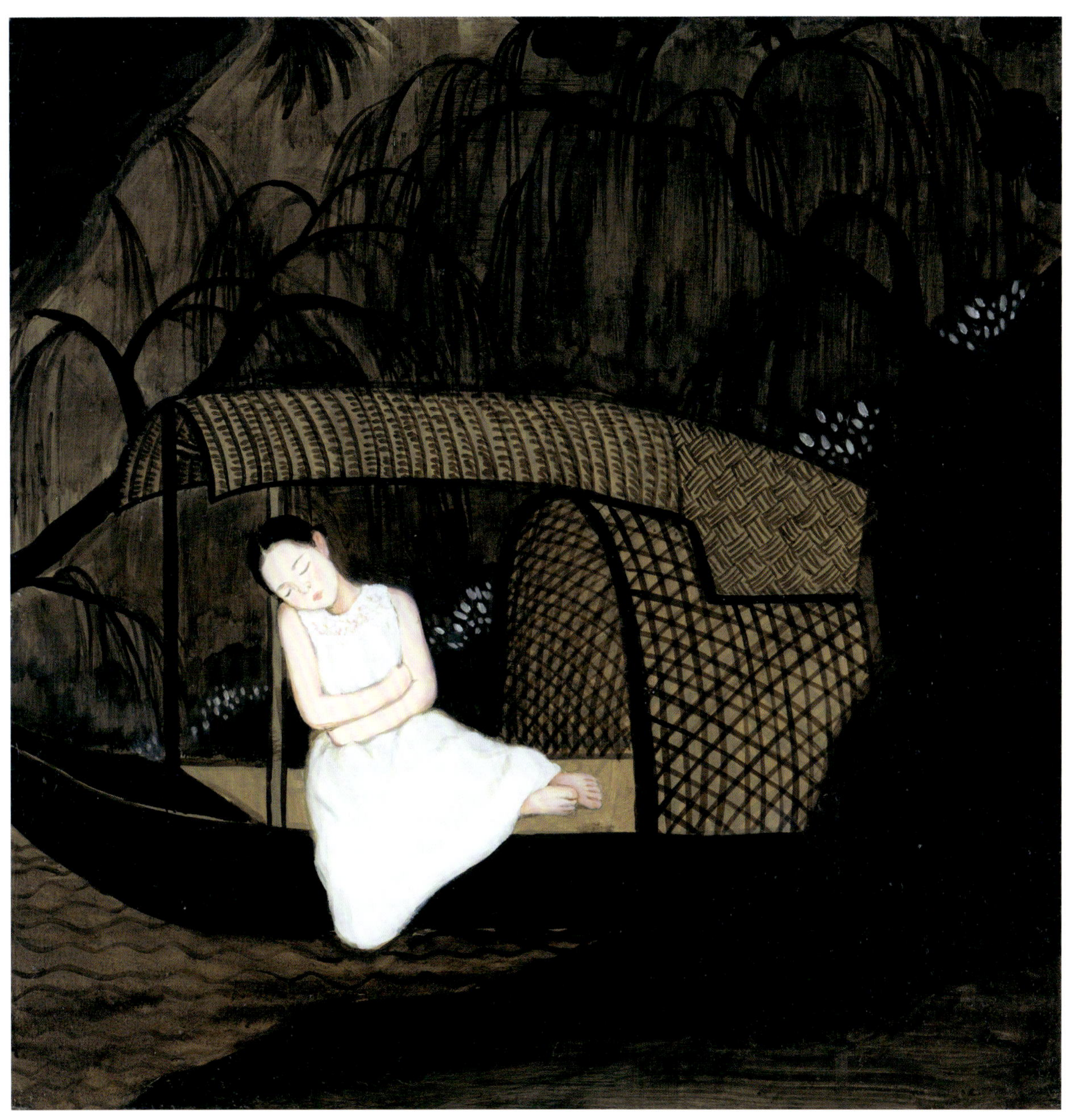

Girl with Boat 004, 2017
30 x 30 cm
Oil on wood

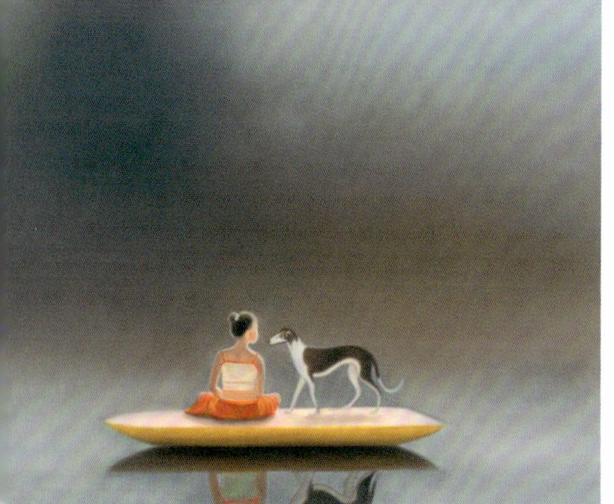

Sanbaishan 21, 2022
50 x 60 cm
Oil on canvas

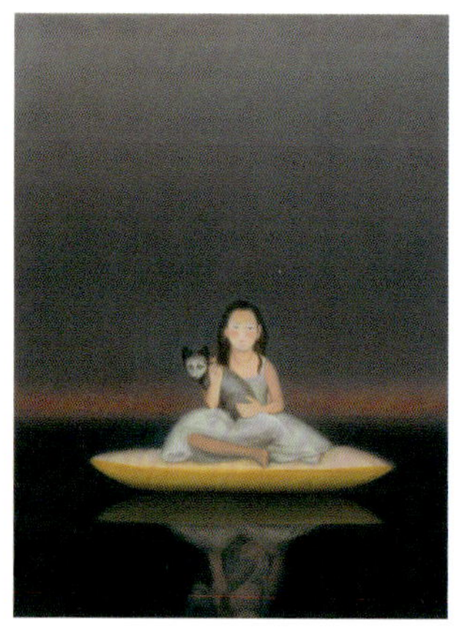

Girl with Boat and Fox 02
2022
40 x 30 cm
Oil on canvas

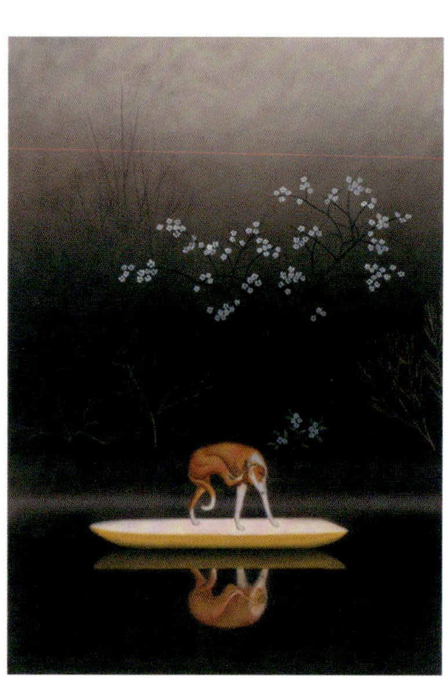

Dog with Boat 01, 2022
70 x 50 cm
Oil on canvas

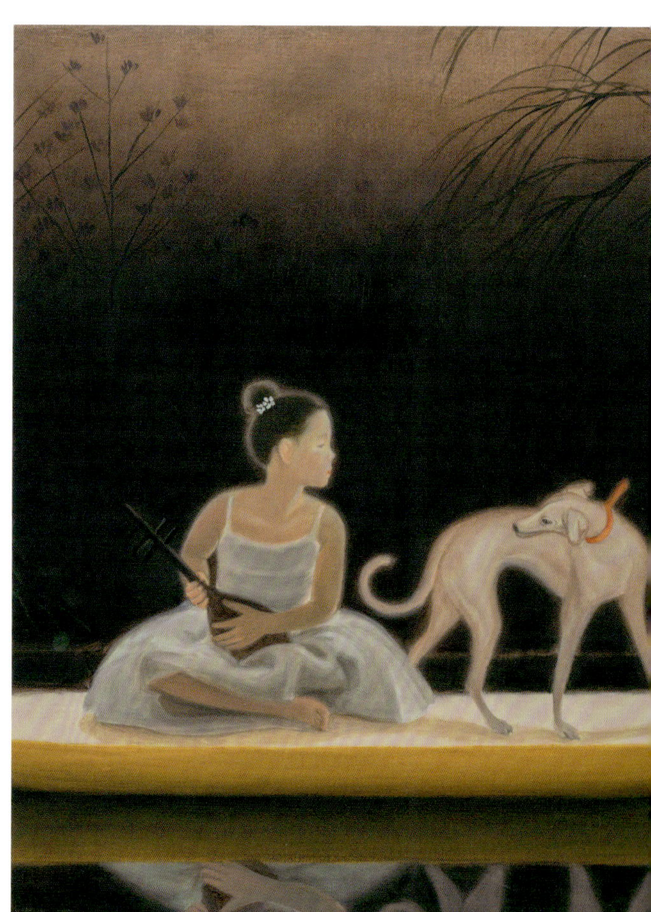

Girl with Dog, 2022
30 x 24 cm
Oil on canvas

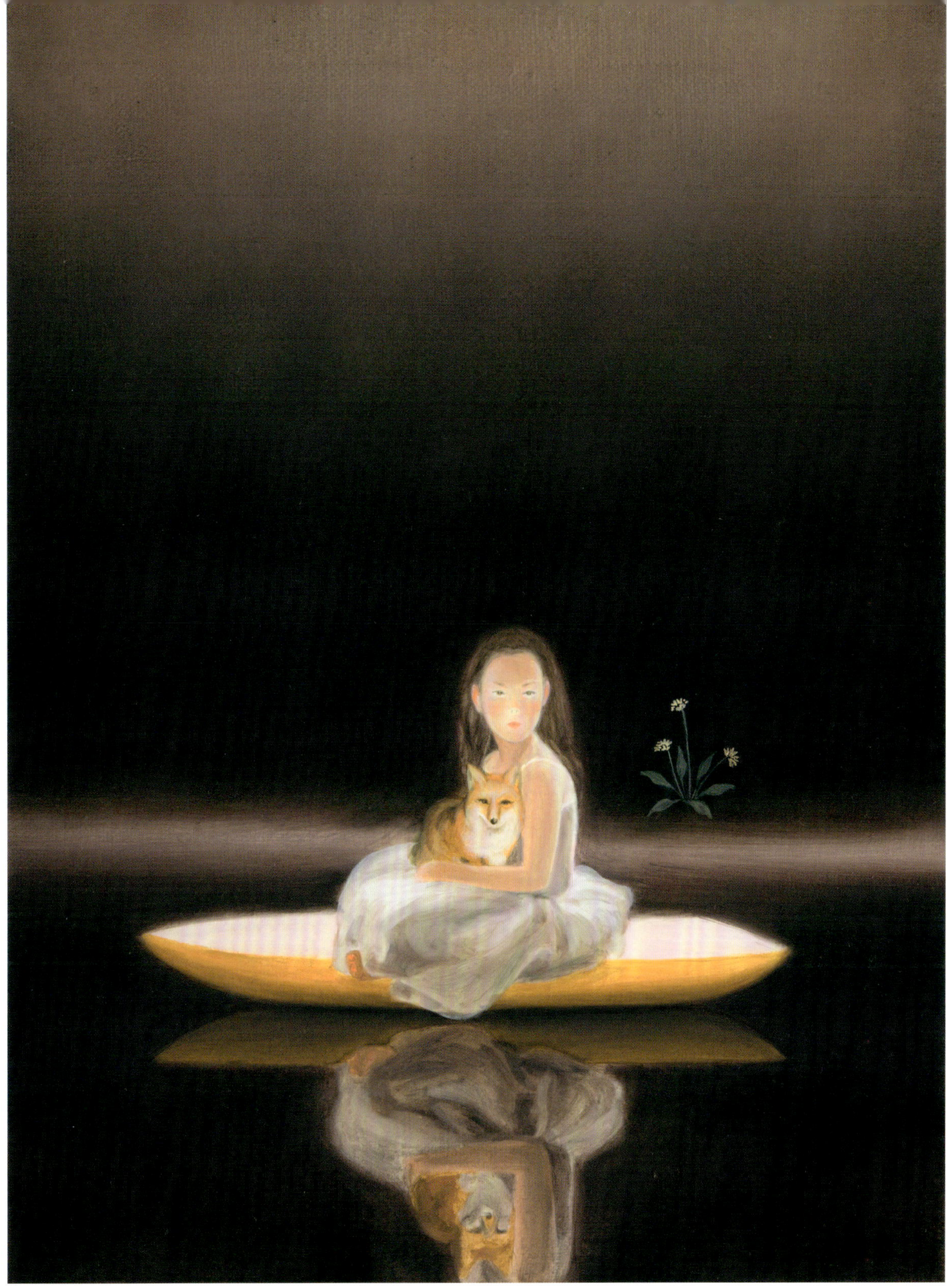

Girl with Boat and Fox 01, 2022
40 x 30 cm
Oil on canvas

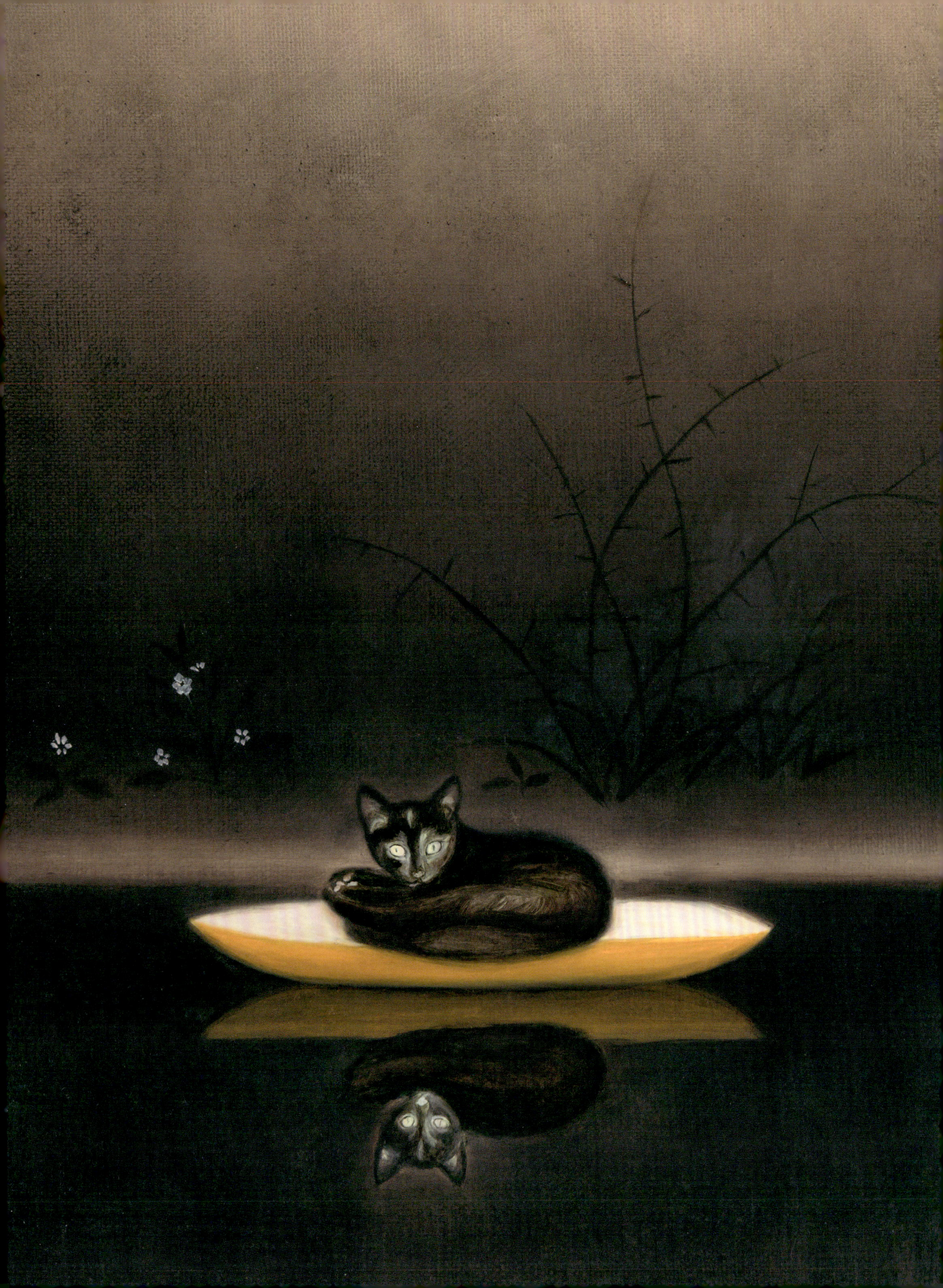

Cat with Boat 02, 2022
40 x 30 cm
Oil on canvas

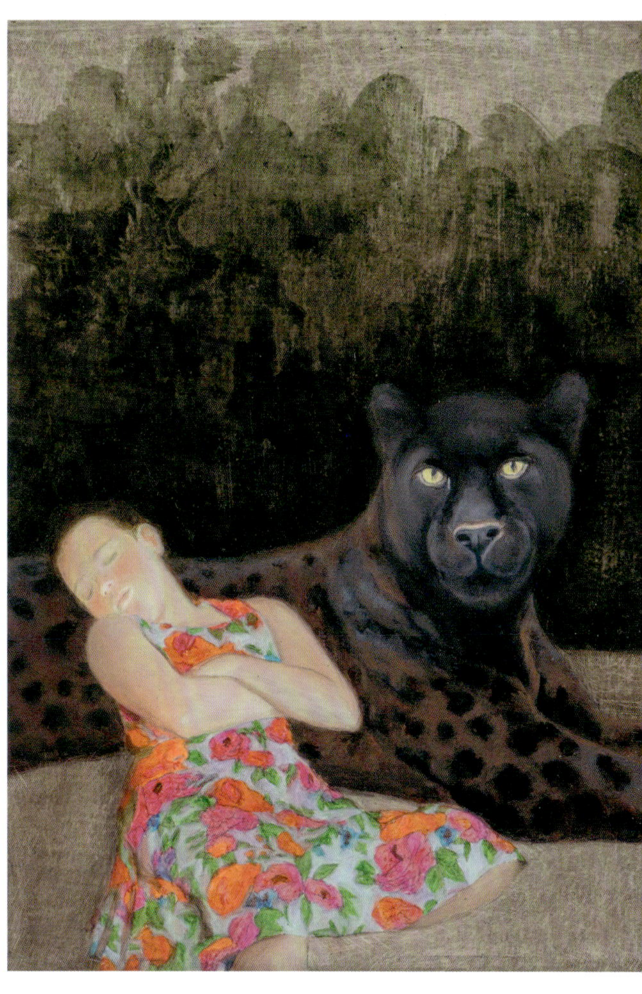

The Journey 15, 2022
24 x 18 cm
Oil on canvas

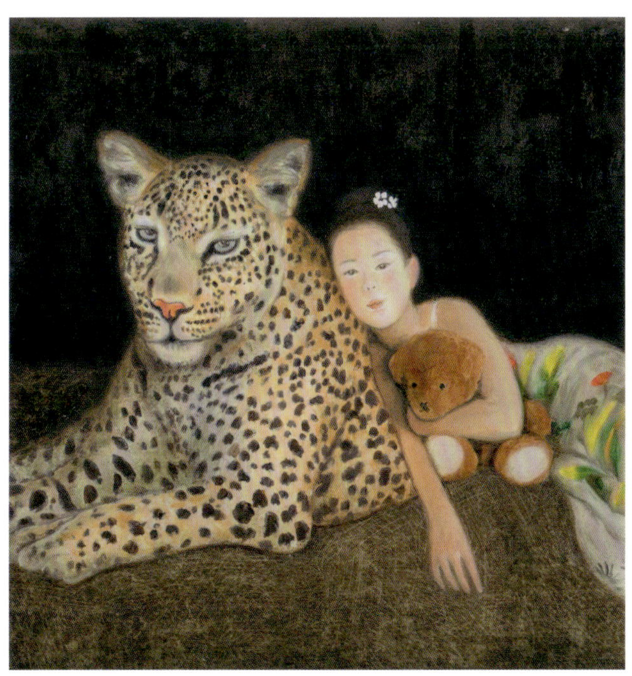

The Journey 16, 2022
20 x 20cm
Oil on canvas

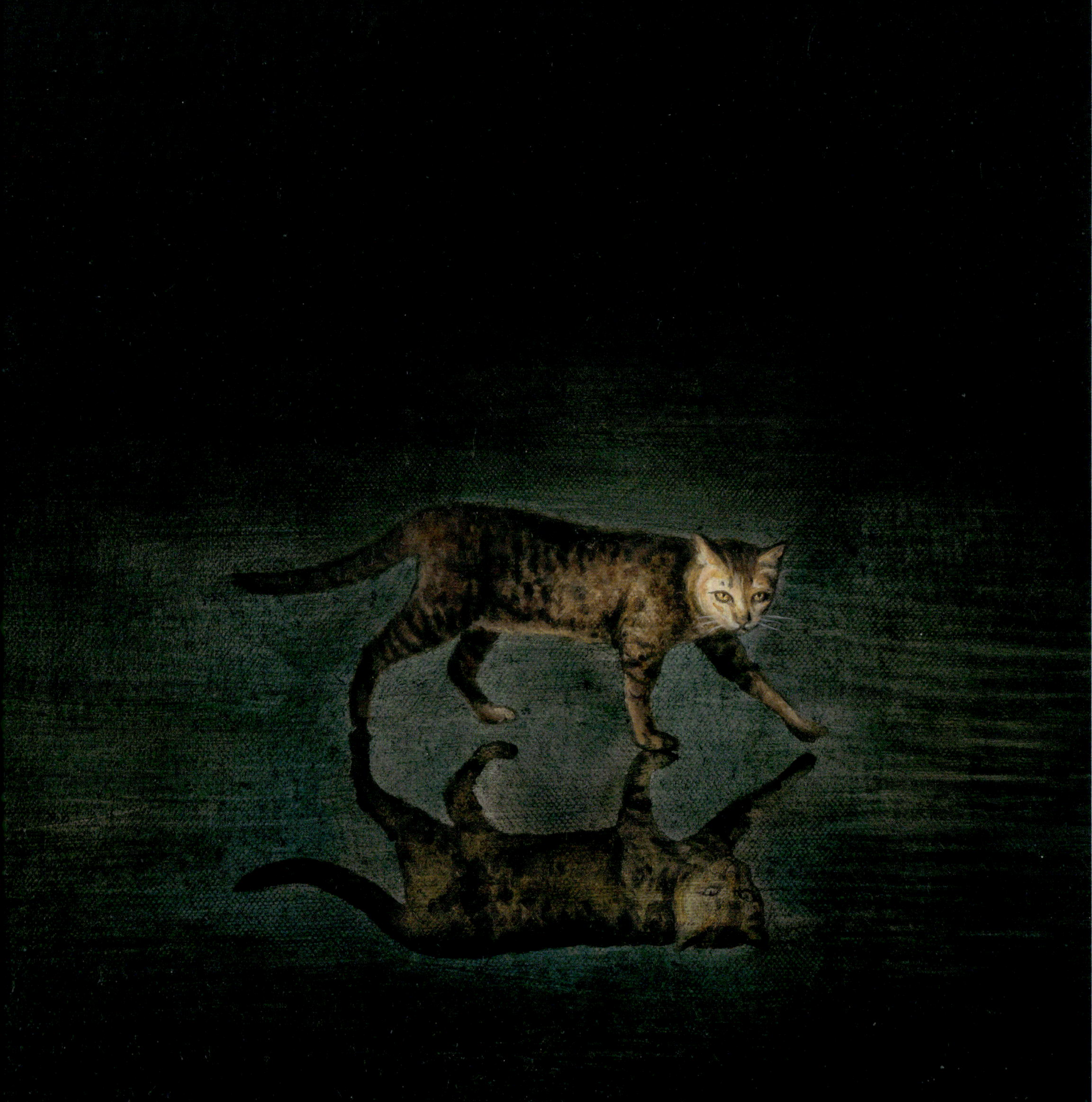

Cat 04, 2022
40 x 30 cm
Oil on canvas

Cat 01, 2022
20 x 15 cm
Oil on canvas

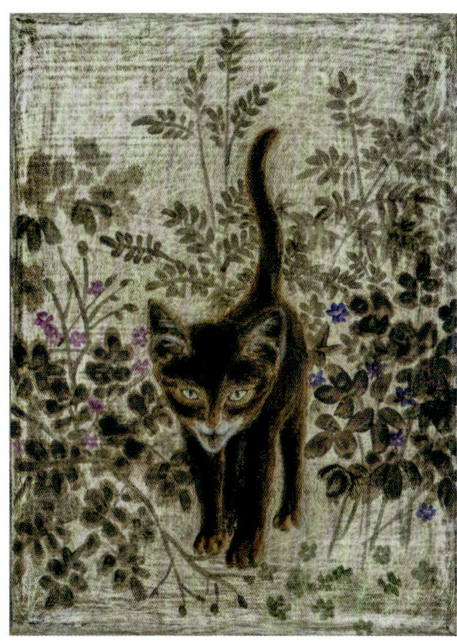

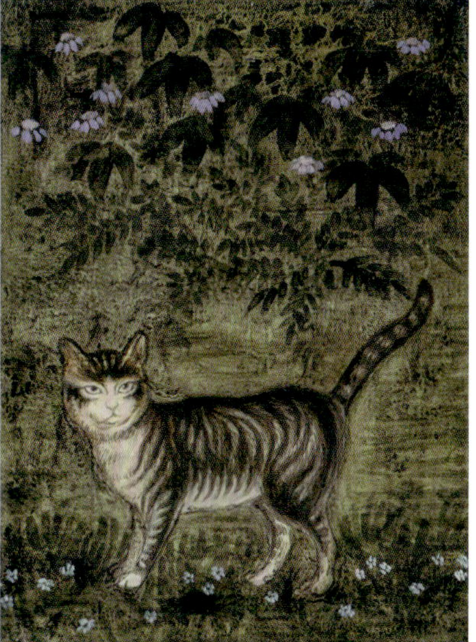

Cat 02, 2022
20 x 15 cm
Oil on canvas

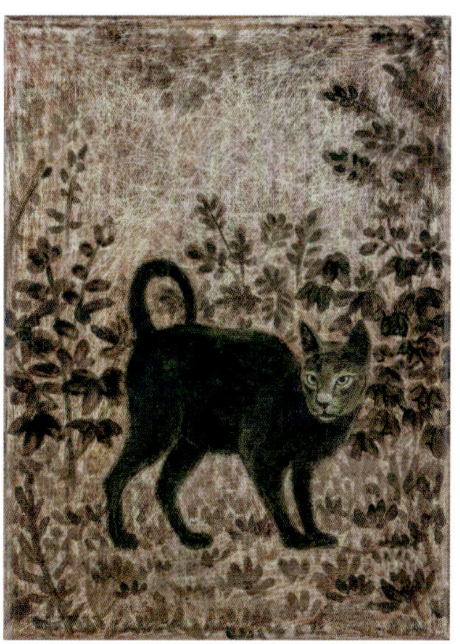

Cat 03, 2022
20 x 15 cm
Oil on canvas

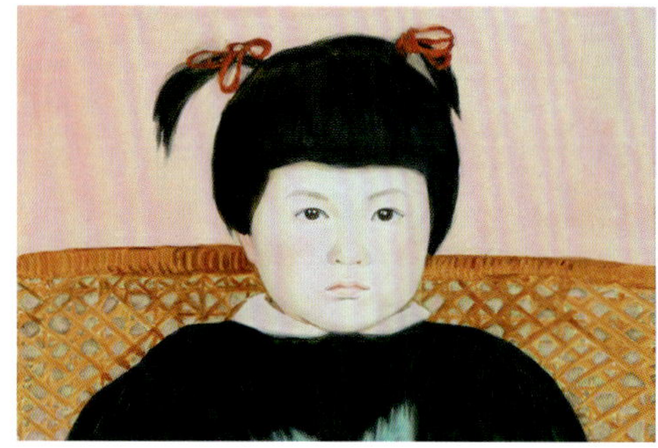

Leilei, 2012
20 x 30 cm
Oil on wood

Be who you are 01, 2013
29,7 x 21 cm
Acrylic on paper

Be who you are 02, 2013
40 x 30 cm
Acrylic on canvas

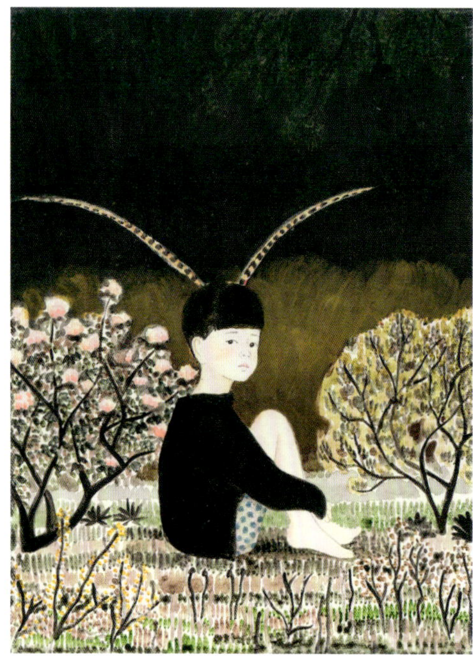

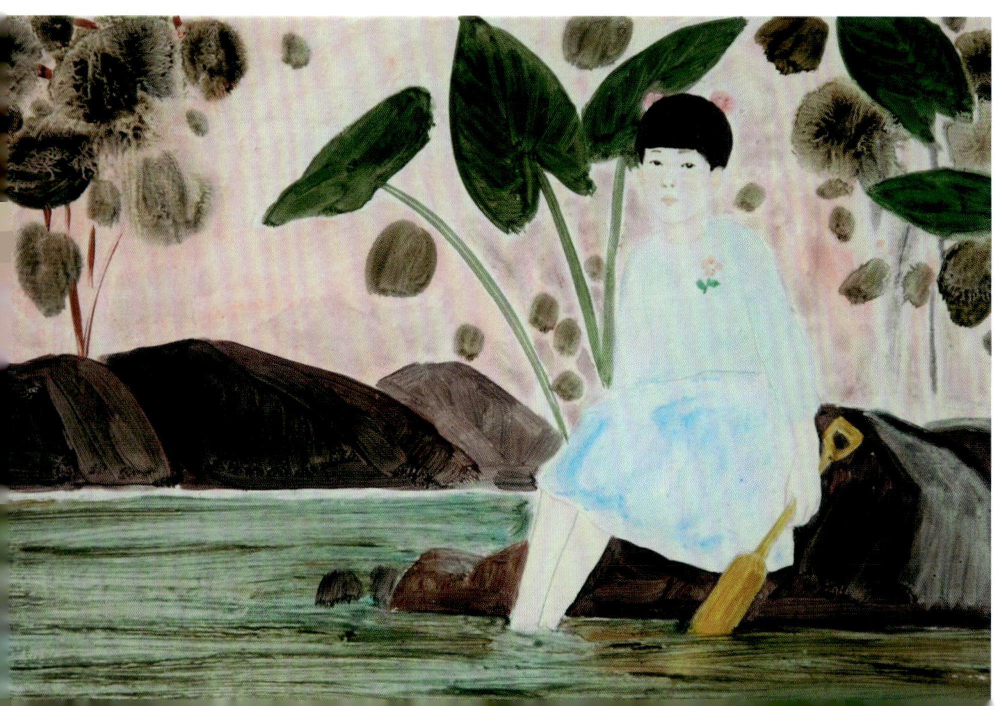

Girl 006, 2011
20 x 30 cm
Oil on wood

Girl 005, 2012
30 x 30 cm
Oil on canvas

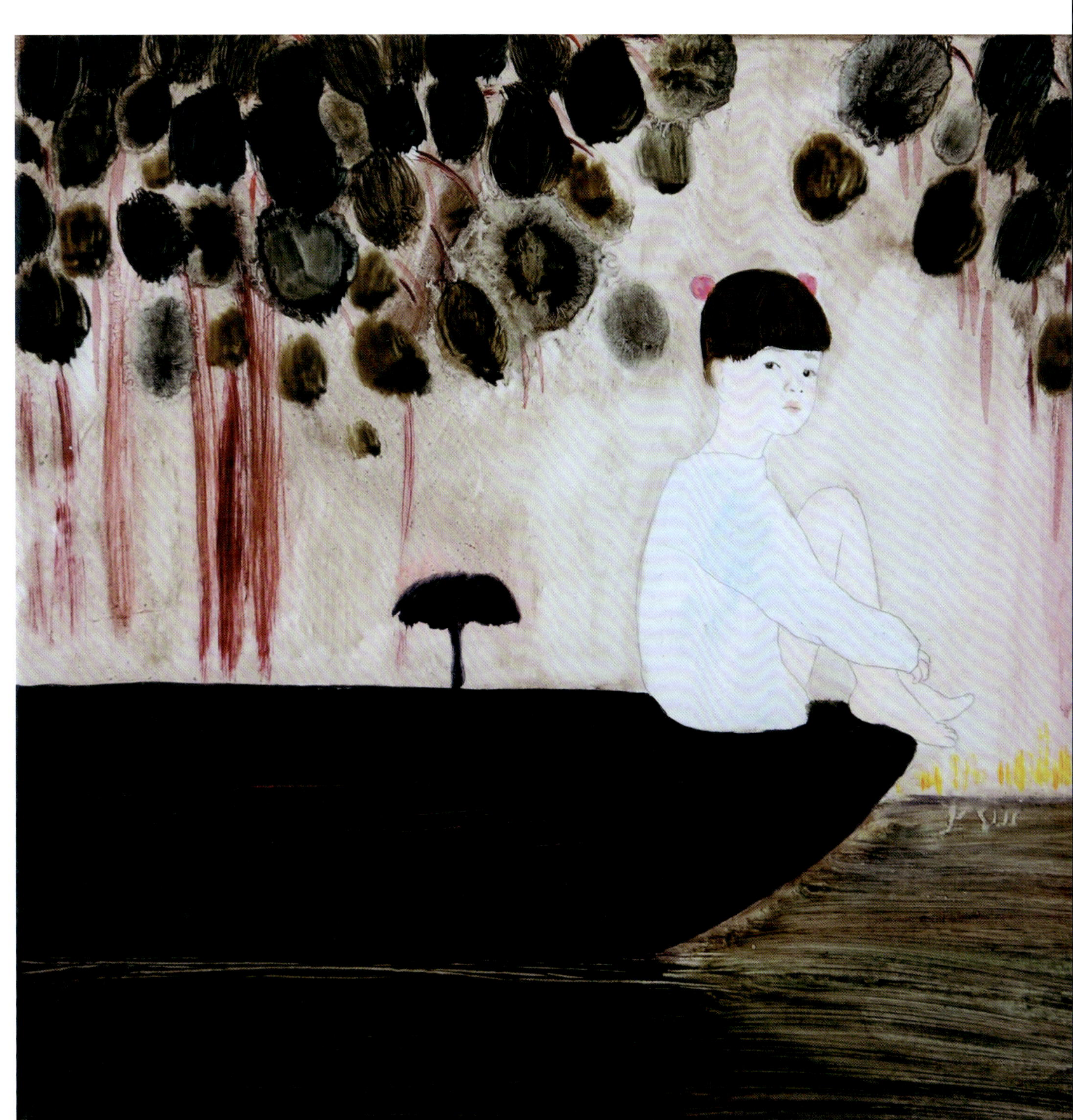

Girl 22, 2013
50 x 50 cm
Acrylic on canvas

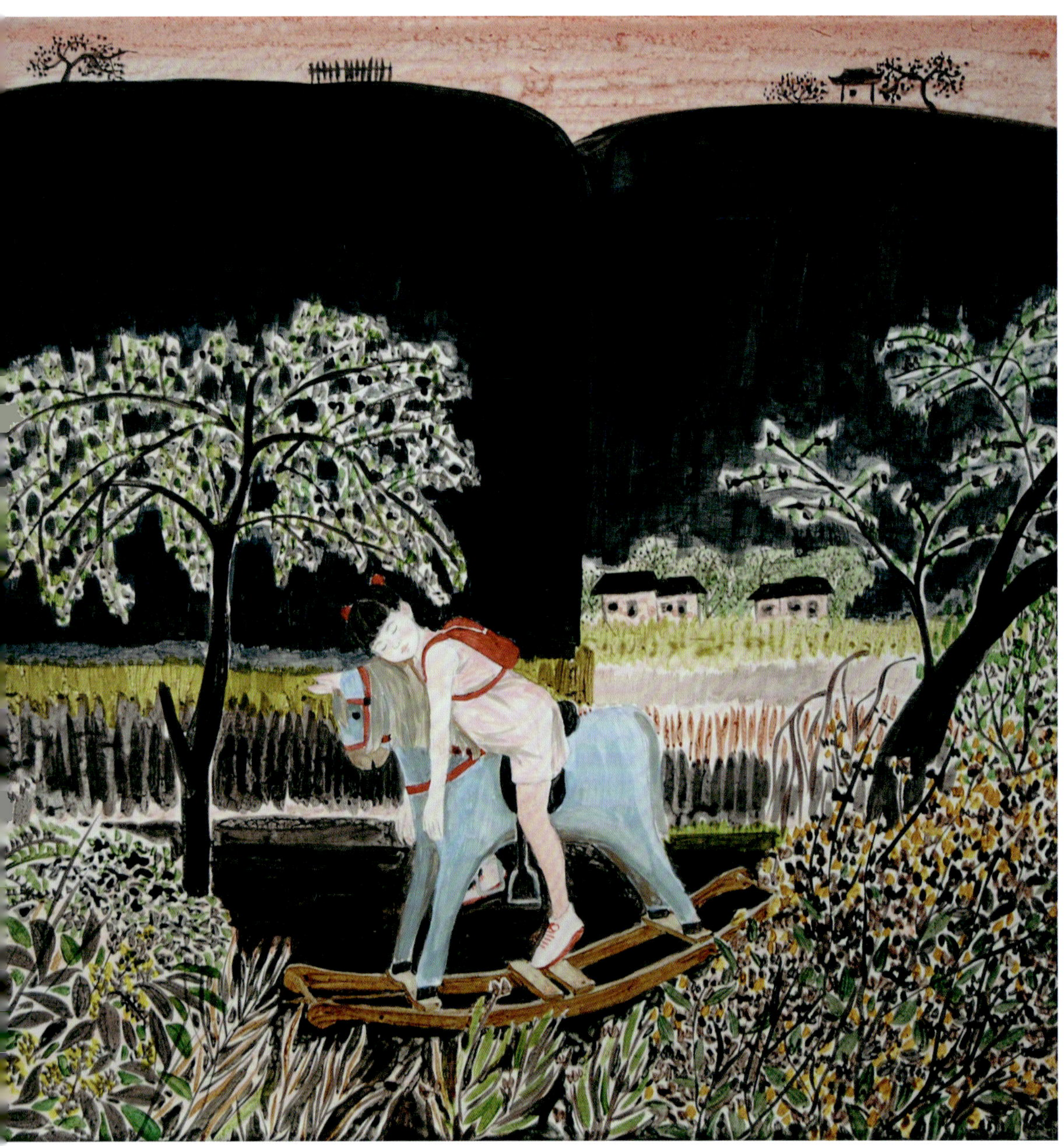

Be who you are 03, 2013
40 x 30 cm
Acrylic on canvas

Girl 19, 2013
30 x 40 cm
Acrylic on canvas

Girl 20, 2013
40 x 40 cm
Acrylic on canvas

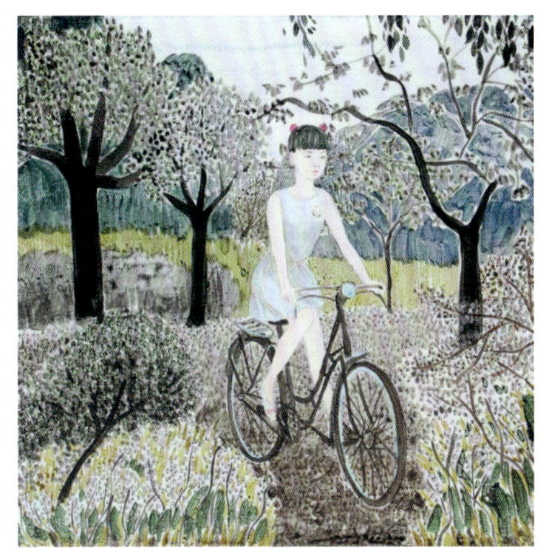

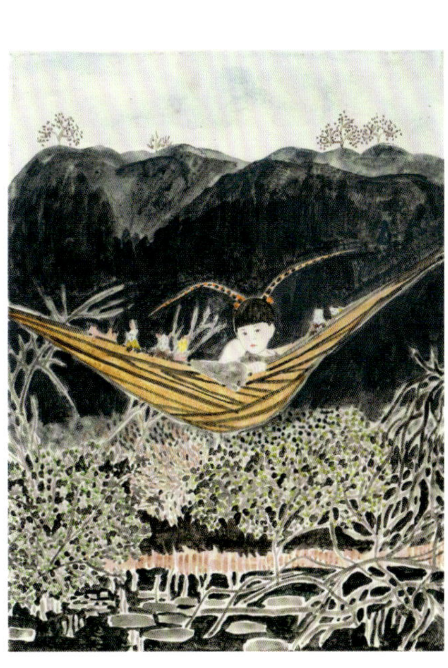

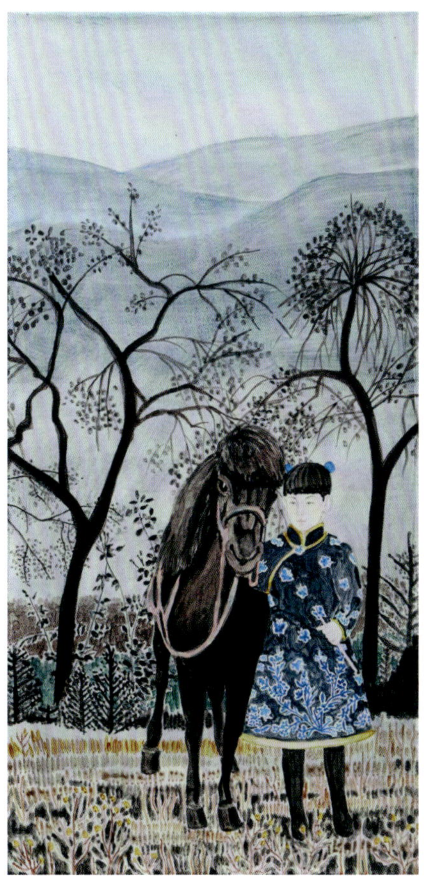

Girl 25, 2013
60 x 30 cm
Acrylic on canvas

Pia 004, 2014
50 x 70 cm
Oil on canvas

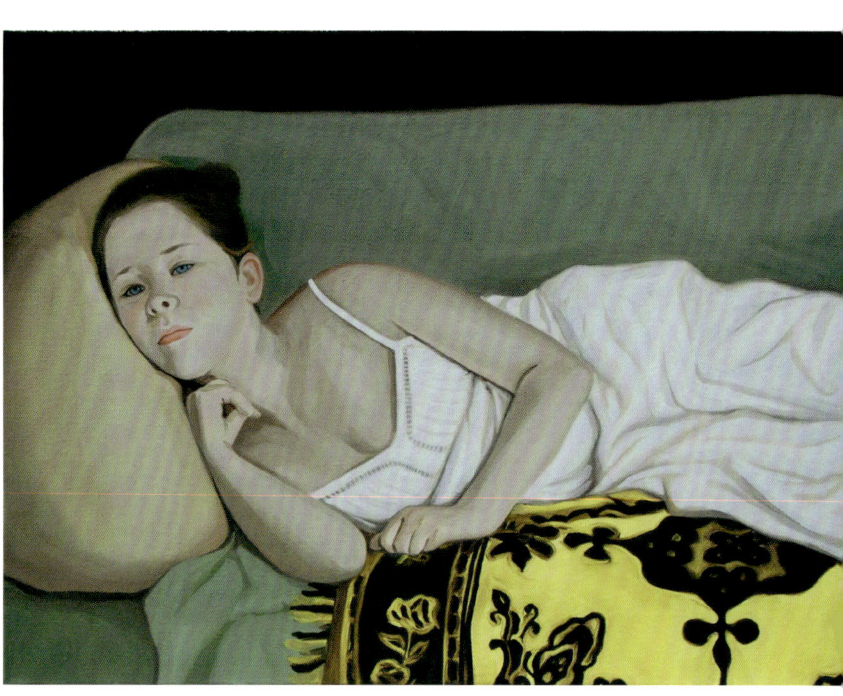

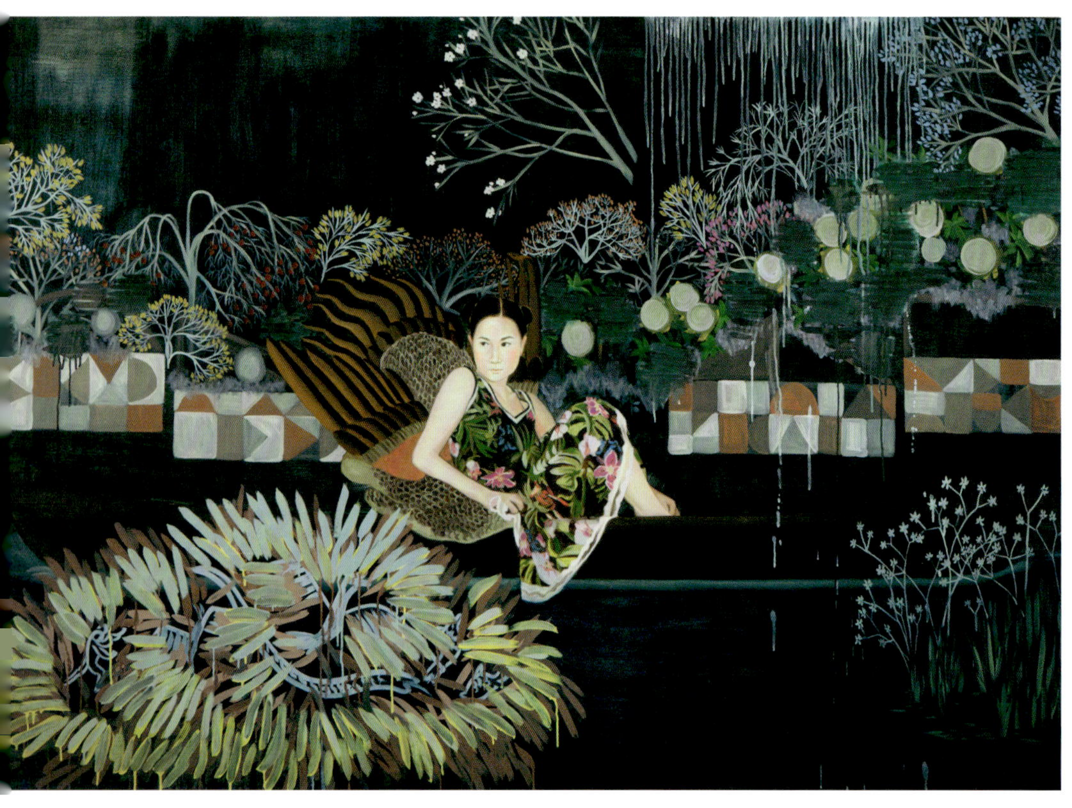

The Journey 07, 2014
130 x 190 cm
Oil on canvas

Girl with Tiger, 2014
70 x 50 cm
Oil on canvas

The Sister 01, 2014
50 x 60 cm
Oil on canvas

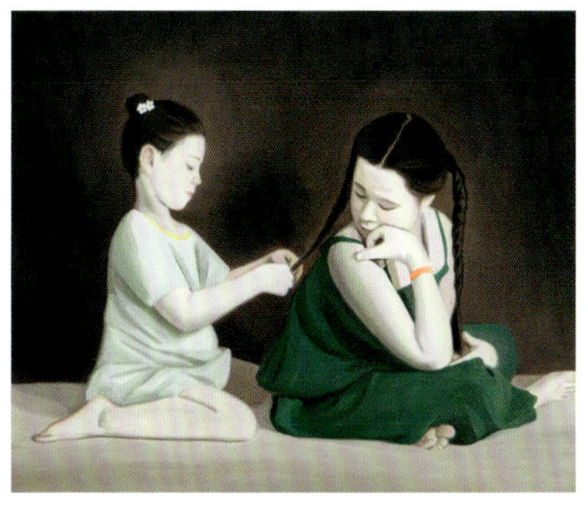

Journey, 2011
190 x 130 cm
Oil on canvas

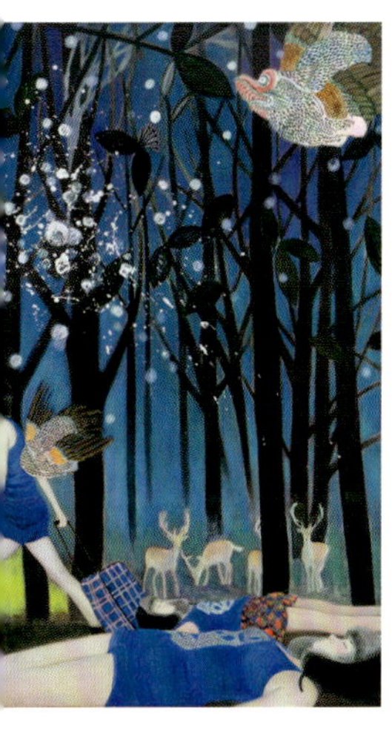

Blossom, 2011
160 x 110 cm
Oil on canvas

Sea Eagle 08, 2011
100 x 80 cm
Oil on canvas

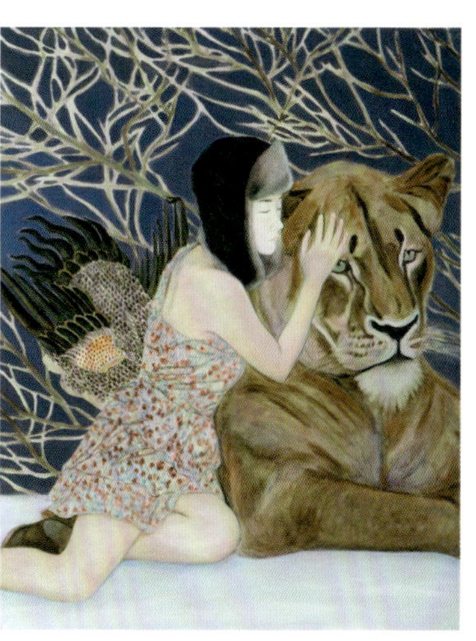

光影之间

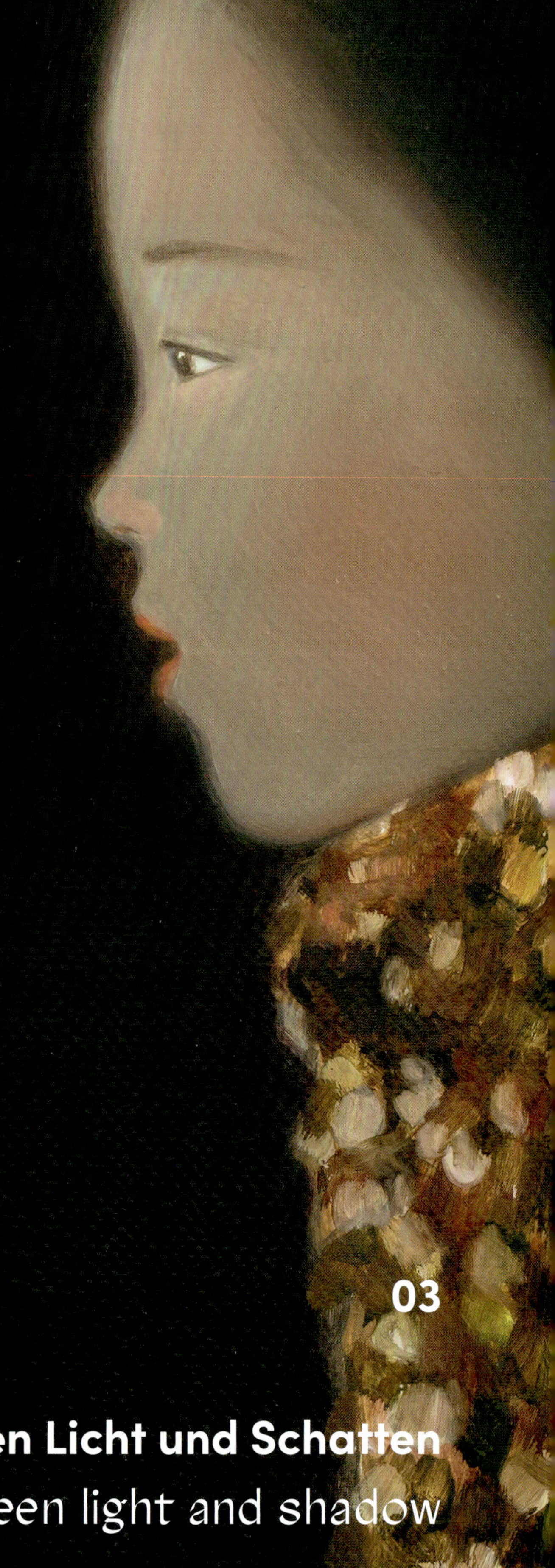

03

Der Raum zwischen Licht und Schatten

The space between light and shadow

Die künstlerische Ideenwelt, in der Haiying Xu nach der Grenze zwischen dem Realen, das sich in ihrer Lebensrealität ereignet hat, und der künstlerischen Vorstellung fragt, verdeutlicht sich in den Werken, die dem Kapitel „Der Raum zwischen Licht und Schatten" zugeordnet sind.

Ihre Malerei ist keine Abbildung des Realen, obwohl sie wie eine Abbildung wirkt. Ihre Malerei ist auch keine illustrative Beschreibung dessen, was es war und wie sie das Ereignis erlebt. Die Kunstwerke von Haiying Xu deuten einen sogenannten dritten Raum an, der ein Zwischenraum zwischen dem Sichtbaren und dem Verborgenen ist.

In der Tat hat Haiying Xu einen Raum gesucht, in dem sie alle Freiheiten hat, den Fragen über die Identität nachzugehen: der von der traditionellen Kultur geprägten Identität, der Identität eines weiblichen Geschlechts im jeweiligen deutschen und chinesischen gesellschaftlichen Kontext und der fluiden Identität einer heranwachsenden jungen Frau, die nach der Antwort auf die Frage sucht, wer sie ist. Mit dieser Freiheit, die das künstlerische Schaffen von Haiying Xu voraussetzt, meine ich eine Befreiung von (Vor-)Urteilen. Die Künstlerin ist nicht ausschließlich als Feministin einzuordnen, als wir über ihre Auseinandersetzung mit weiblichen Identitäten sprachen. Als europäischer Rezipient kann man von der Kunst Haiying Xus nicht erwarten, dass sie, wie ihre Zeitgenossen, eindeutig politisch Stellung bezieht. Für Haiying Xu darf Kunst nicht instrumentalisiert werden, um Meinungen in diesem visuellen Medium auszudrücken. Vielmehr interessiert sie das Offene, das Formbare in ihrem künstlerischen Prozess.

Paul Klee hat einmal gesagt, dass die Kunst nicht das Sichtbare wiedergibt, sondern das Unsichtbare sichtbar macht. Dieser Kunstbegriff Klees verbindet sich mit dem bildnerischen Denken von Haiying Xu. Die Künstlerin modelliert den unsichtbaren dritten Raum in ihren Werken, indem sie das traditionelle Schattenspiel verfremdet. Sie löst die Figuren aus diesem geschichtlichen Kontext des Schattenspiels heraus. Was wir hier sehen, sind keine abgebildeten Schattenspiele, keine visuellen Erzählungen historischer Abläufe, sondern ein von Haiying Xu eröffneter dritter Raum. In diesem geht sie intuitiv der Frage nach, wie sie ihre Fantasie in einer Begegnung mit den Figuren aus dem Schattenspiel umgesetzt hat.

Das Schattenspiel（皮影戏）, auch chinesisches Schattentheater genannt, ist eine der bedeutendsten Kunstformen der chinesischen Kunsttradition. Im Jahr 2011 wurde das chinesische Schattentheater in die Repräsentative Liste des immateriellen Kulturerbes der Menschheit der UNESCO aufgenommen. Das Besondere an diesem Spiel ist eine halbtransparente Trennwand, die als Bühne dient. Die zweidimensionalen, meist aus Leder gefertigten und aufwendig bemalten und gestalteten Puppenfiguren werden von den Spielern mit an den Figuren befestigten Stöcken bewegt. Die Trennwand fungiert dabei als Projektions- und Rezeptionsfläche. Die Wand trennt das Publikum vom Theater; gleichzeitig trennt sie das Licht, das von der Seite der Spieler kommt, von seinem Schatten, in dem die Geschichte lebendig dargestellt wird. Dieses Verhältnis zwischen Licht- und Schattenspiel, die die Einzigartigkeit des chinesischen Schattentheaters ausmacht, kann als Ausgangspunkt für die in diesem Kapitel vorgestellten Arbeiten gesehen werden. Die Verhältnisse von Hell-Dunkel, Licht-Schatten, Aktiv-Passiv, An- und Abwesenheit, die im Werk der Künstlerin durch dieses Schattenspiel erzeugt werden, sind das eigentliche Thema der künstlerischen Gestaltung. In dieser Werkgruppe „der Raum zwischen Licht und Schatten" zeigt die Künstlerin den Bewusstseinszustand eines träumenden Mädchens. Damit wird der Prozess des Träumens beleuchtet, der sich ebenfalls in Verhältnissen zwischen realen Gegebenheiten und gedanklichen Erweiterungen abspielt. Die Schweizer Psychoanalytikerin Verena Kast schrieb in ihrem Buch „Der Schatten in uns", dass der Umgang mit dem Schatten als eine typische menschliche Aufgabe anzuerkennen ist. Denn nach ihrer Auffassung ist dort, wo Menschen sind, auch immer mit Schatten zu rechnen. Diesen Schatten zu integrieren, indem man seinen Blick auf ihn wirft, bedeutet nach Kast nicht, ihn hemmungslos auszuleben, sondern zu akzeptieren, dass es ihn gibt.

Durch diesen integralen Verarbeitungsprozess, der ohne Vorstellungskraft nicht möglich ist, gelingt es dem Menschen, sich bewusst zu sein und den Bezug zum eigenen Schatten herzustellen. Dieser Schatten repräsentiert das Unsichtbare oder das Unbekannte, das im Unbewussten liegt. Nach der Auffassung des Schweizer

Psychiaters C.G. Jung müsse der Schatten nichts Moralisch-Verwerfliches bedeuten, sondern könne durchaus gute Qualitäten beinhalten wie Instinkte, wirklichkeitsgetreue Wahrnehmungen oder schöpferische Impulse. Die Bezugnahme erfolgt persönlich, individuell und frei, was besonders bei heranwachsenden Frauen zu beobachten ist, deren Imaginationspotential eine hohe Dynamik aufweist. Erst durch diese Imagination wird den jungen Frauen bewusst, was Identität ist und wie sie entsteht.

Die leise Spannung, die Haiying Xu in diesem Kapitel auf Grundlage ihres autobiografischen Hintergrunds aufbaut, stellt uns vor die Frage: Wie können wir Freiheit schaffen, ohne den Kontakt zu unserer Welt zu verlieren? Mehr Zeit zum Träumen könnte der erste Schritt in diese Richtung sein. Denn den Traum bezeichnete Sigmund Freud als Königsweg des Unbewussten. Ein Traum entspricht einer freien Wahrnehmung. Er lässt sich von der physischen Realität nicht einschränken. Träume unterliegen weder den Gesetzen der Physik noch gesellschaftlichen Konventionen und Zwängen. Träume entstehen nur aus uns selbst heraus. Sie sind privat und einmalig; aber gleichzeitig magisch und fantasievoll. Aus dieser Quelle der individuellen Fantasie schöpft Haiying Xu immer wieder traumhafte Bilder.

The artistic realm of ideas, in which Haiying Xu questions where to draw the line between real-life occurrences and artistic imagination, becomes clear in the works that have been allocated to the chapter "The space between light and shadow".

Her paintings are not a depiction of the real, although they may seem like one. Her work is also not an illustrative description of that which has happened and how she experienced the event. The works of art by Haiying Xu hint at a so-called "third space", which is an in-between space twixt the visible and the concealed.

In fact, Haiying Xu looked for a space in which she has complete freedom to pursue questions of identity: that of an identity shaped by traditional culture, the identity of the female sex within the context of German and Chinese societies respectively and the fluid identity of the adolescent young woman who questions who she really is. By this "freedom", which the artistic work of Haiying Xu assumes, I mean liberation from (pre-) judgement. The artist is not to be classified exclusively as a feminist when we speak of her exploration of female identities. As a European recipient of her work, one cannot expect Haiying Xu's art to have a clear political standpoint like that of her contemporaries. For Haiying Xu, art should not be instrumentalized to express opinions through this visual medium. She is far more interested in that which is open and malleable in her artistic process.

Paul Klee once said, "Art does not reproduce the visible but makes visible." Klee's concept of art is connected to Haiying Xu's artistic thinking. The artist models the invisible third space in her works, in which she defamiliarizes the traditional shadow play. She releases the characters from the historical context of the shadow play. Here, we do not see depictions of shadow plays or visual accounts of historical events, but rather a third space, called into being by Haiying Xu. In this space, she intuitively asks how her imagination has dealt with her encounter with the shadow play characters.

The shadow play(皮影戏), also called Chinese shadow theatre, is one of the most significant art forms of Chinese artistic tradition. In 2011, the Chinese shadow theatre was included in UNESCO's Representative List of the Intangible Cultural Heritage of Humanity. The exceptional thing about the shadow play is the semi-transparent dividing wall, which serves as a stage. The two-dimensional puppets, which are mostly made out of leather, lavishly painted and carefully formed are moved by the puppeteers using the sticks that are attached to the figures. The dividing wall functions as a screen for the projection and reception of the shadows. The wall divides the audience from the drama. At the same time, it separates the light, which comes from the side of the puppeteers, from its shadow, through which the story is portrayed. This relationship between the play of light and shadow, which makes Chinese shadow theatre so unique, can be seen as the point of departure for the works presented in this chapter. The relationships between light and dark, light and shadow, active and passive, presence and absence, which are created in the work of the artist, are the actual theme of the artistic composition. In this group of artworks, "The space between light and shadow", the artist shows the consciousness of a dreaming girl. In this way she highlights the process of dreaming, which also plays with the relationship between real situations and conceptual enhancements of them. The Swiss psychoanalyst Verena Kast wrote in her book The Shadow in Us (Der Schatten in Uns) that shadow-interaction is recognizable as a typical human task. For, as she sees it, wherever there are people, shadows are also to be expected. According to Kast, the integration of this shadow into one's being by gazing at it does not mean its uninhibited expression, but rather the acceptance of its existence.

Through this integral fabrication process, which is impossible without the power of imagination, people succeed in becoming conscious of themselves and creating a connection with their own shadow. This shadow represents the invisible or the unknown that lies in the realm of the unconscious. According to Swiss Psychiatrist C.G. Jung, the shadow does not necessarily signify anything morally reprehensible, but rather could be composed of thoroughly good qualities like instincts, realistic perceptions or creative impulses.2 The reference is personal, individual and free, which is particularly noticeable in adolescent women, whose imaginative potential is extremely dynamic. Young women only become conscious of what identity is and how it comes about through this capacity to imagine.

The subtle tension, which Haiying Xu builds upon the foundation of her autobiographical background in this chapter, begs the following question: How can we create freedom without losing contact with our world? The first step in this direction could be to spend more time dreaming. After all, Sigmund Freud defined the dream as the ideal way to access the unconscious. A dream is equal to a freedom of perception. It is not restricted by physical reality. Dreams do not abide by the laws of physics or social conventions and constraints. Dreams emerge directly from ourselves. They are private and unique, but magical and imaginative at the same time. Haiying Xu continues to create dreamlike pictures from the source of her own individual imagination.

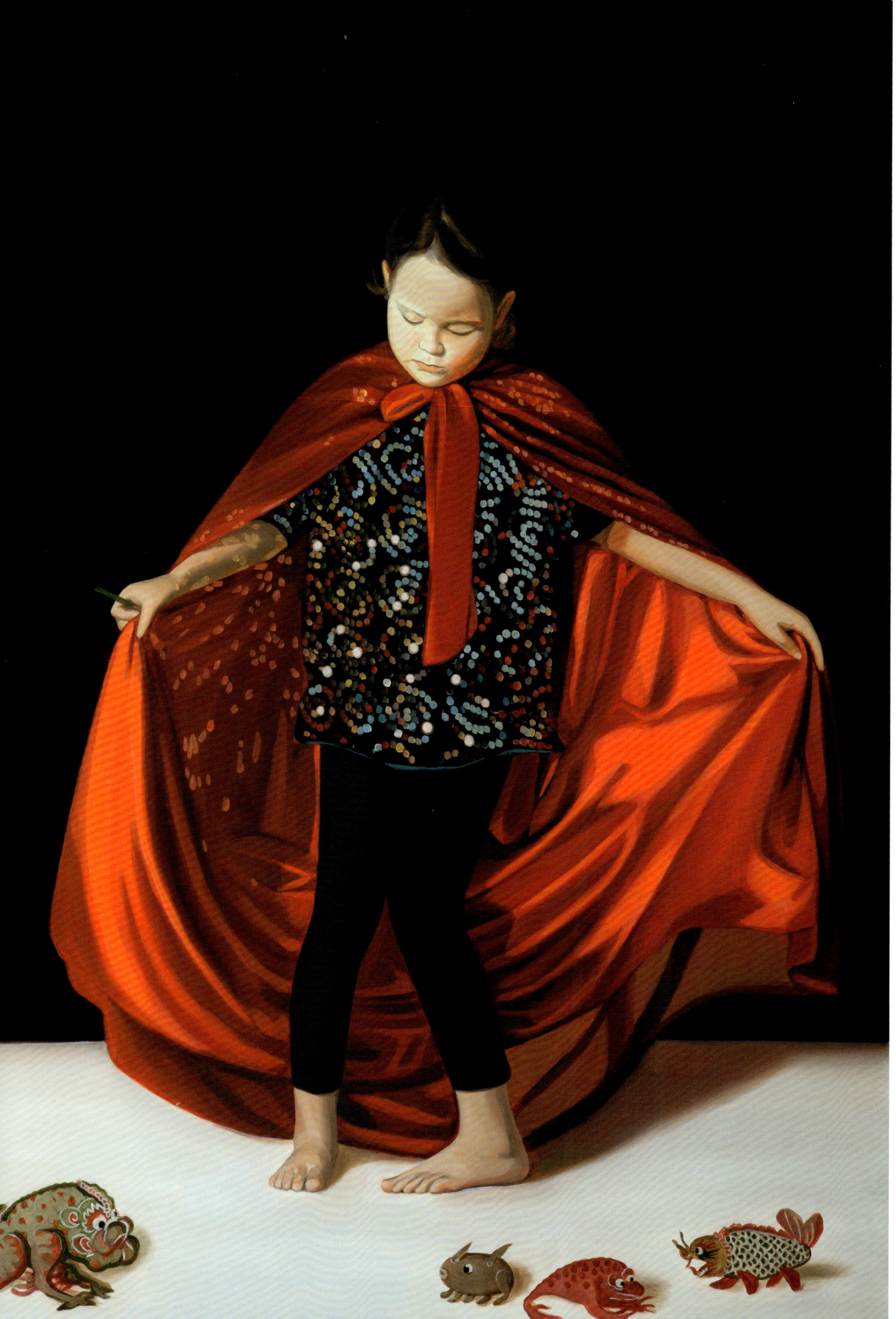

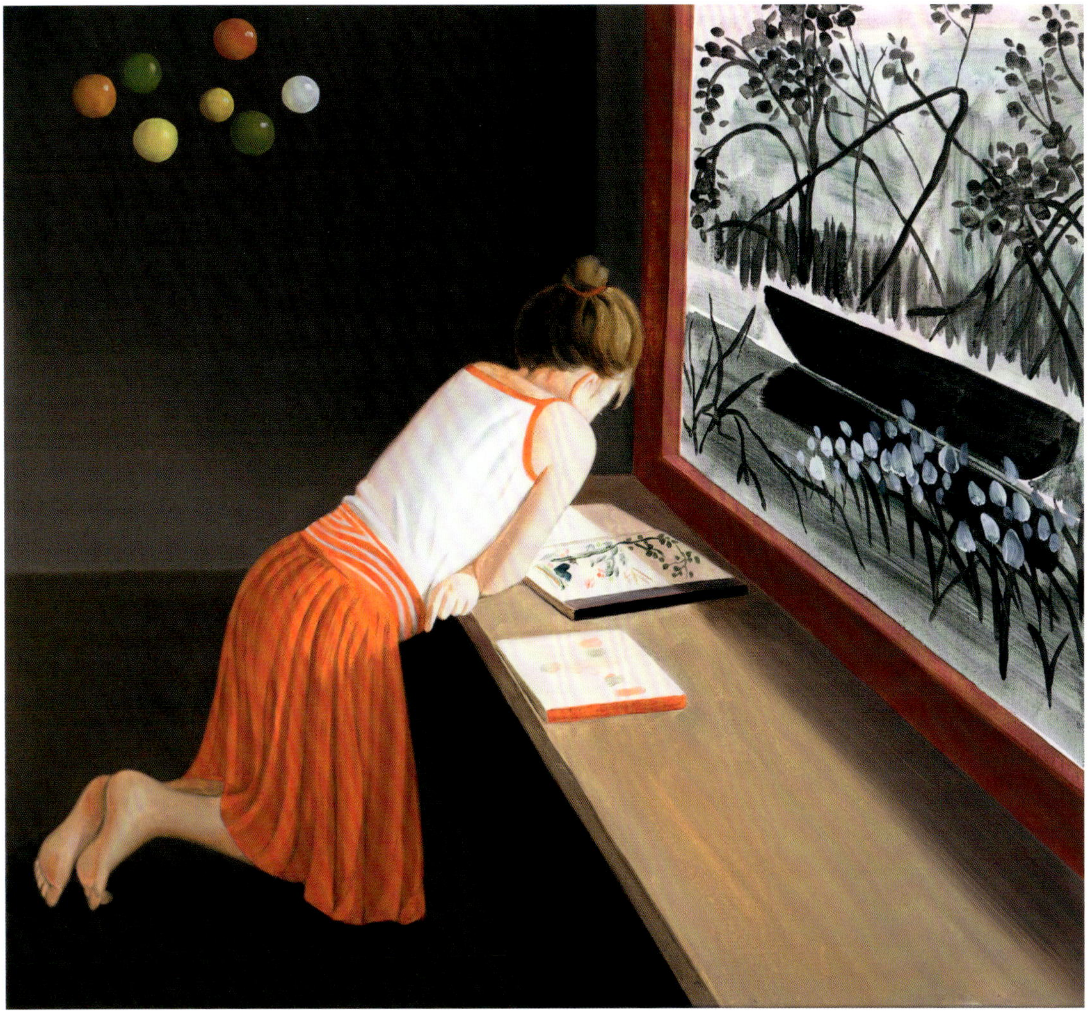

Once Upon a Time 007, 2015
90 x 100 cm
Oil on canvas

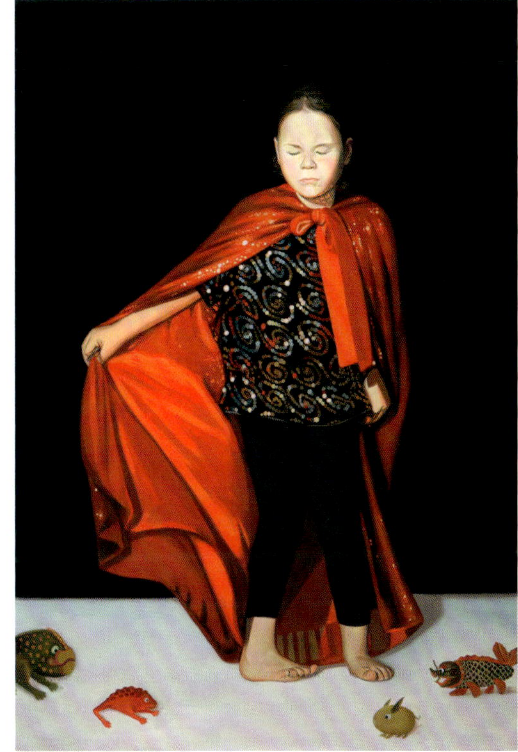

Once Upon a Time 008
2015
100 x 70 cm
Oil on canvas

Once Upon a Time 011
2016
100 x 70 cm
Oil on canvas

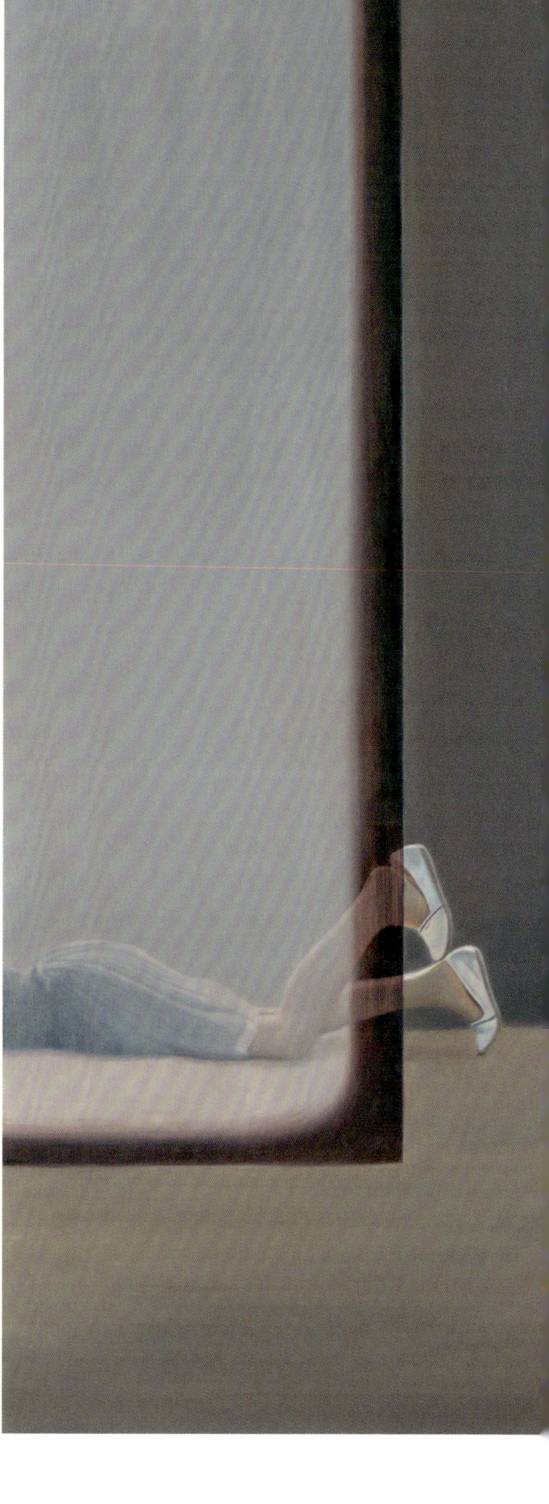

Once Upon a Time 013
2016
80 x 120 cm
Oil on canvas

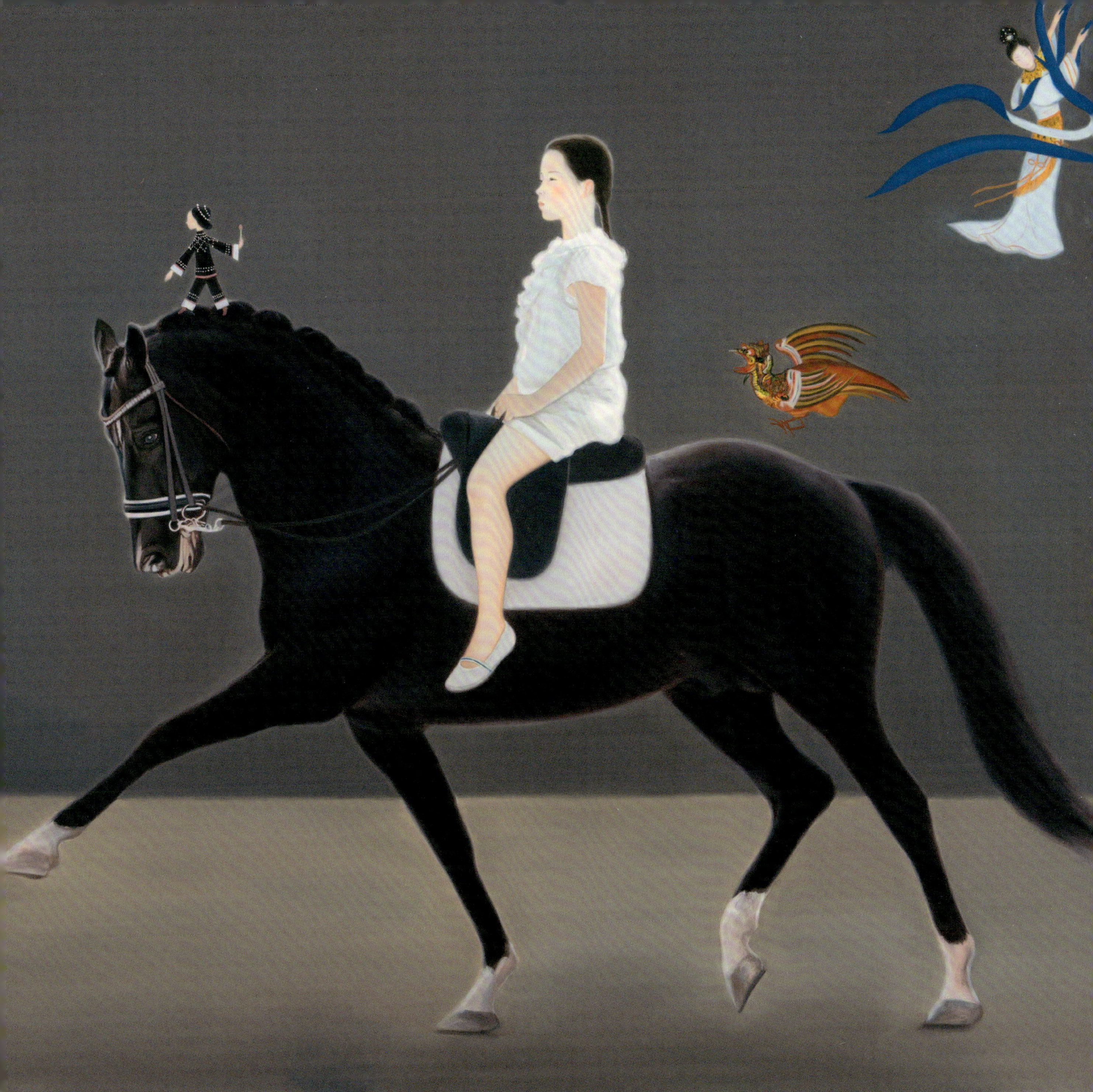

Once Upon a Time 014
2021
110 x 160 cm
Oil on canvas

Once Upon a Time 006 with Dragon, 2015
100 x 70 cm
Oil on canvas

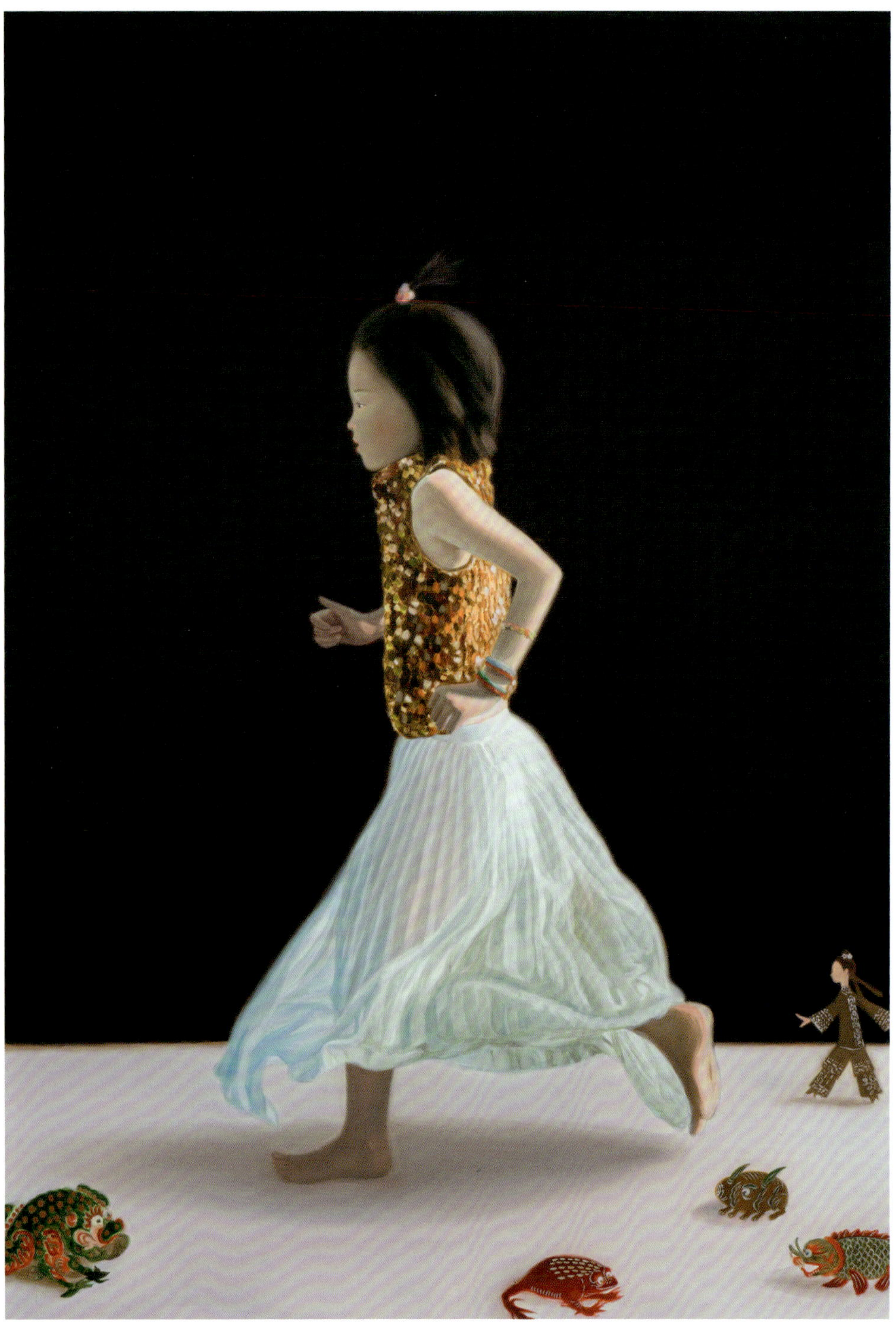

I am a Cloud 05, 2023
100 x 70 cm
Oil on canvas

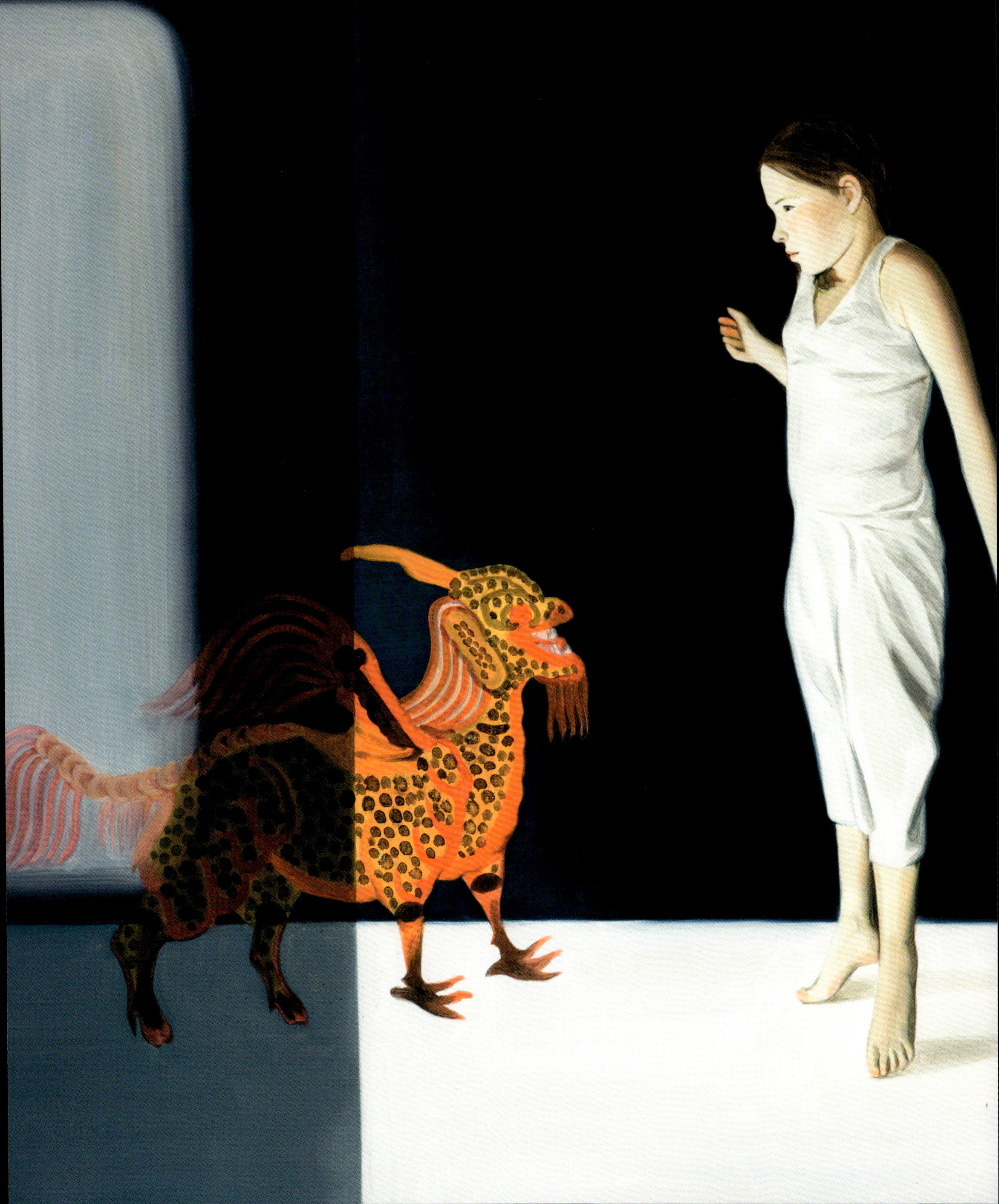

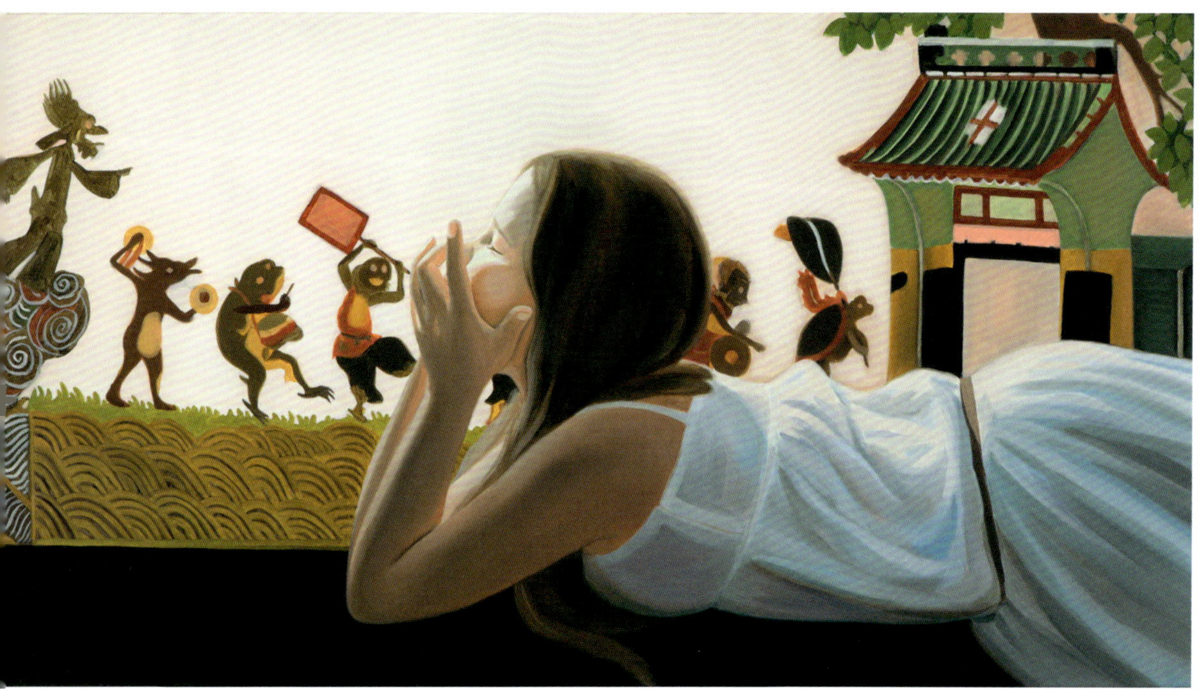

Once Upon a Time 005, 2015
60 x 110 cm
Oil on canvas

Once Upon a Time 004, 2015
110 x 160 cm
Oil on canvas

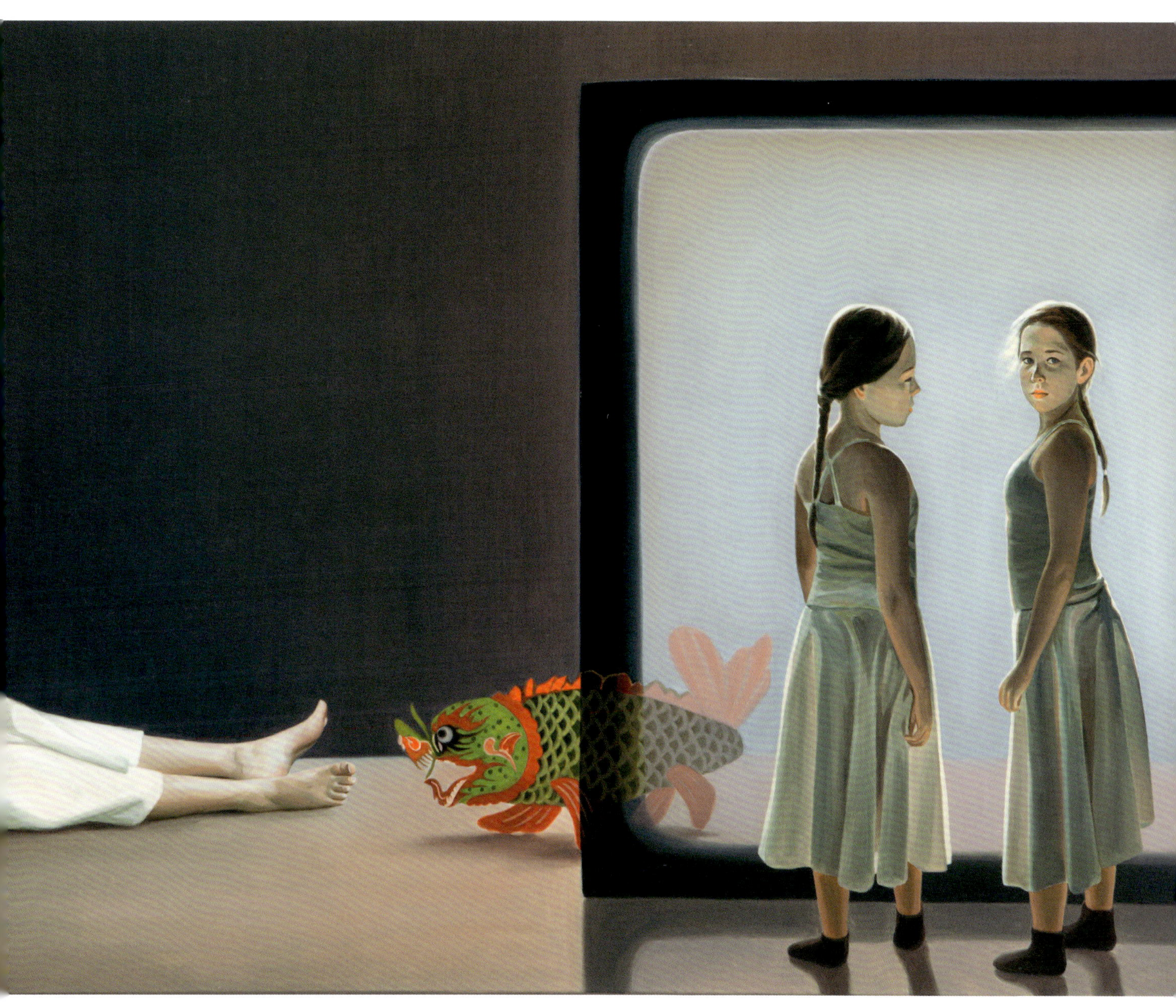

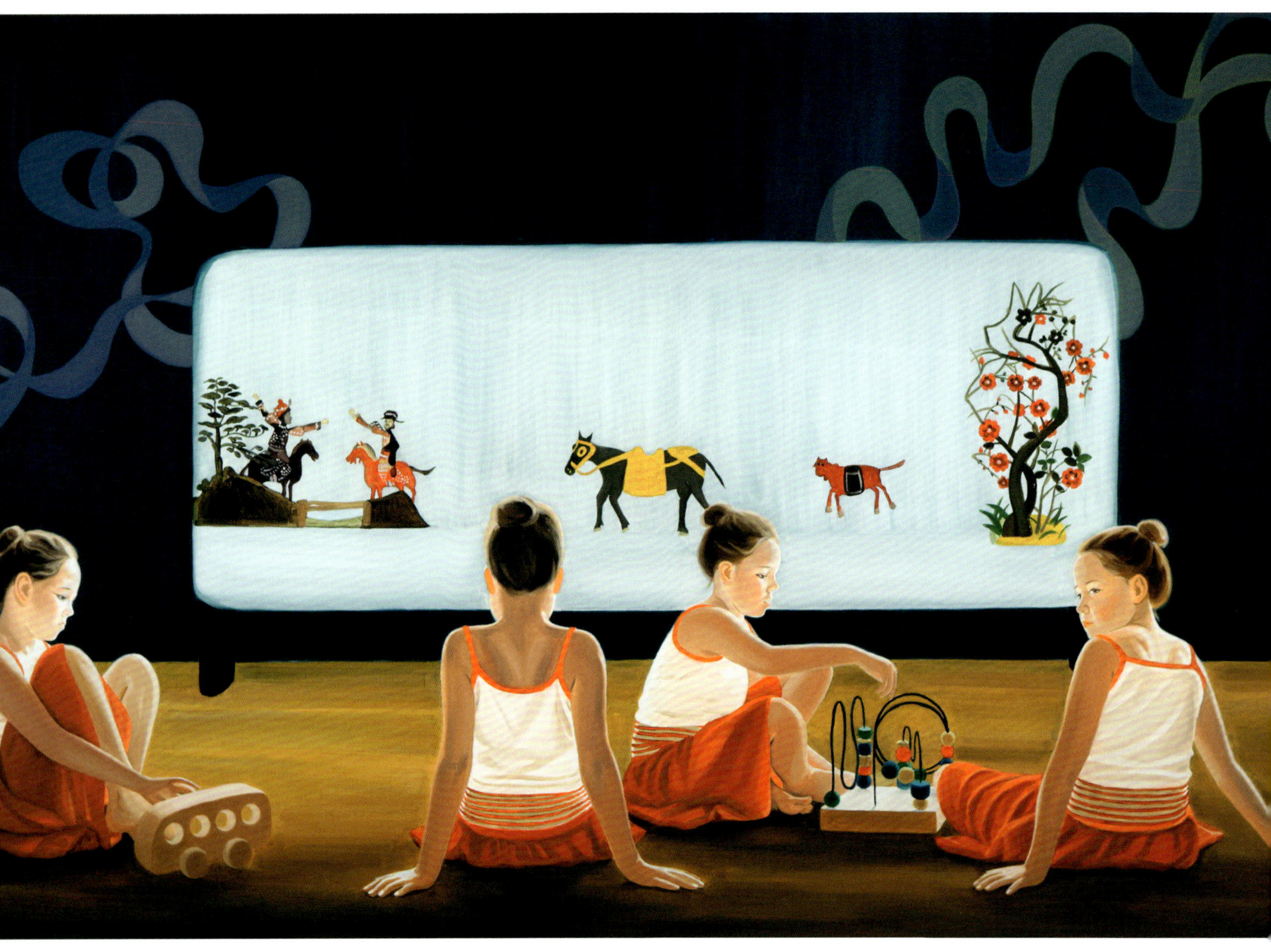

Once Upon a Time 003, 2015
110 x 160 cm
Oil on canvas

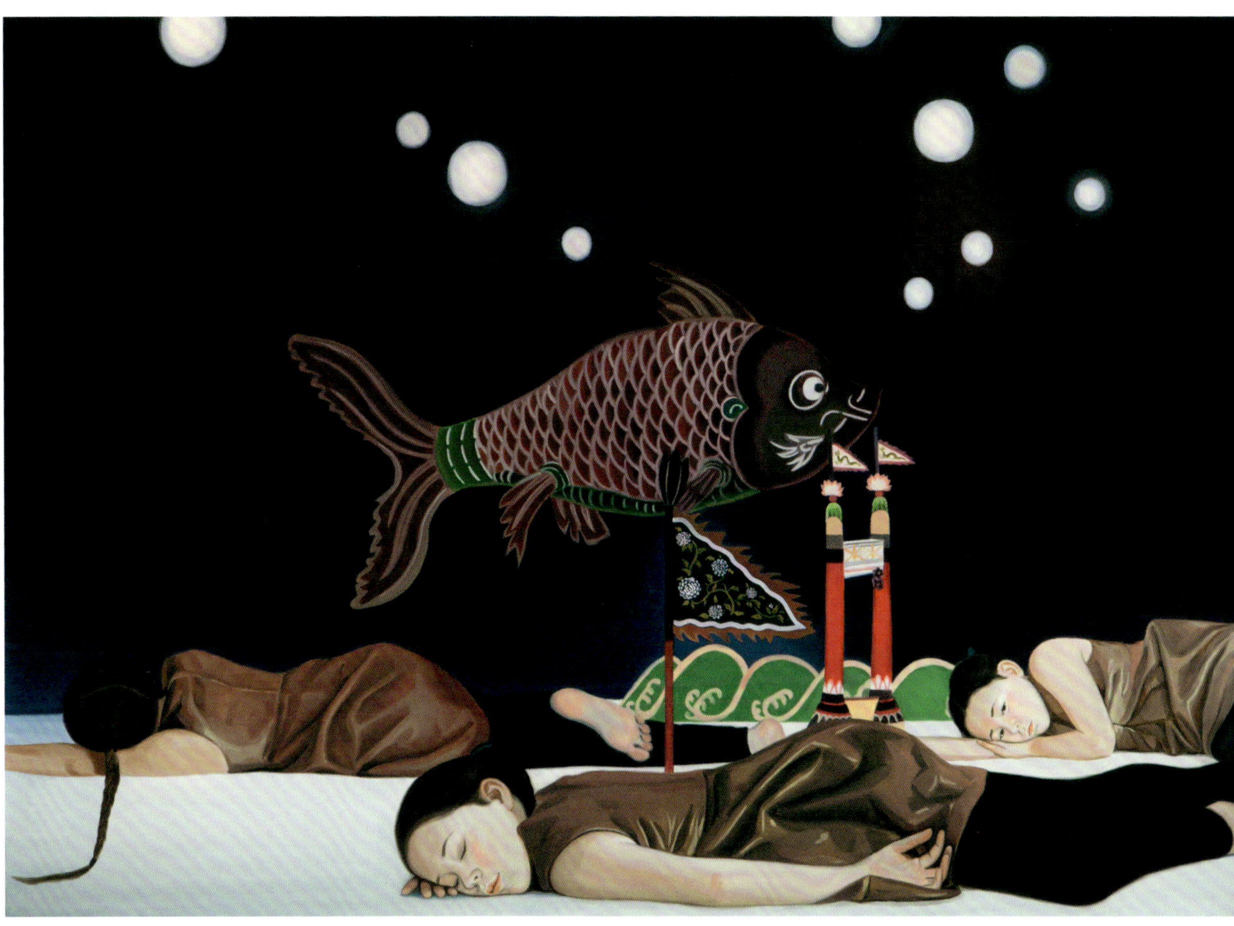

The Journey 10, 2015
110 x 160 cm
Oil on canvas

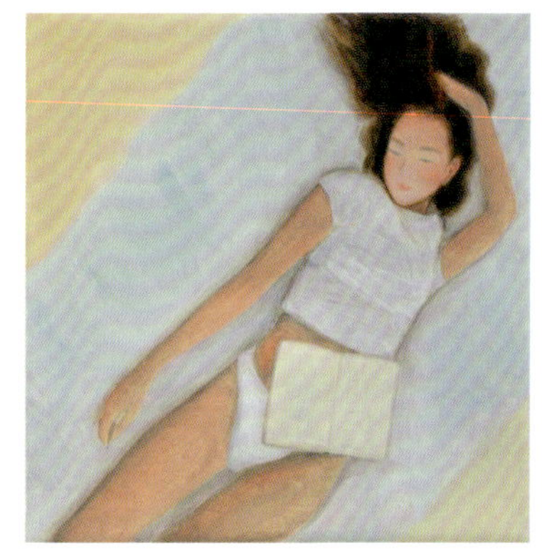

I am a Cloud 03, 2023
20 x 20 cm
Oil on canvas

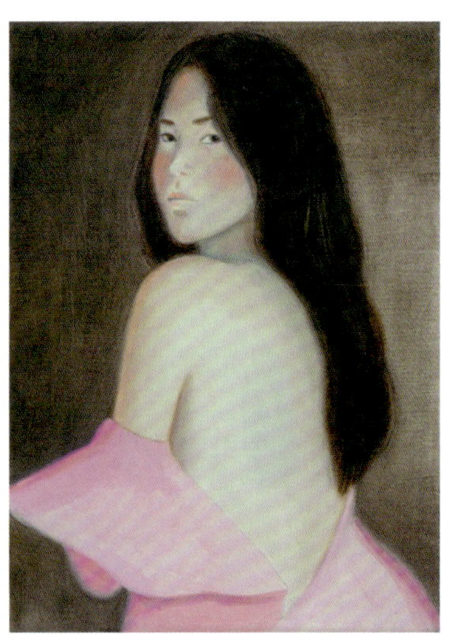

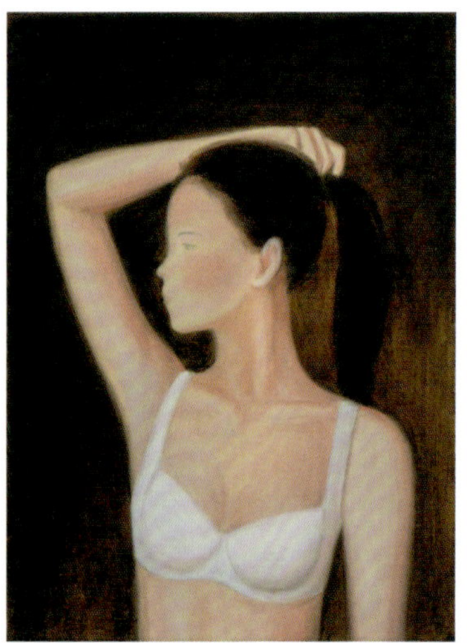

I am a Cloud 01, 2023
24 x 18 cm
Oil on canvas

I am a Cloud 02, 2023
24 x 18 cm
Oil on canvas

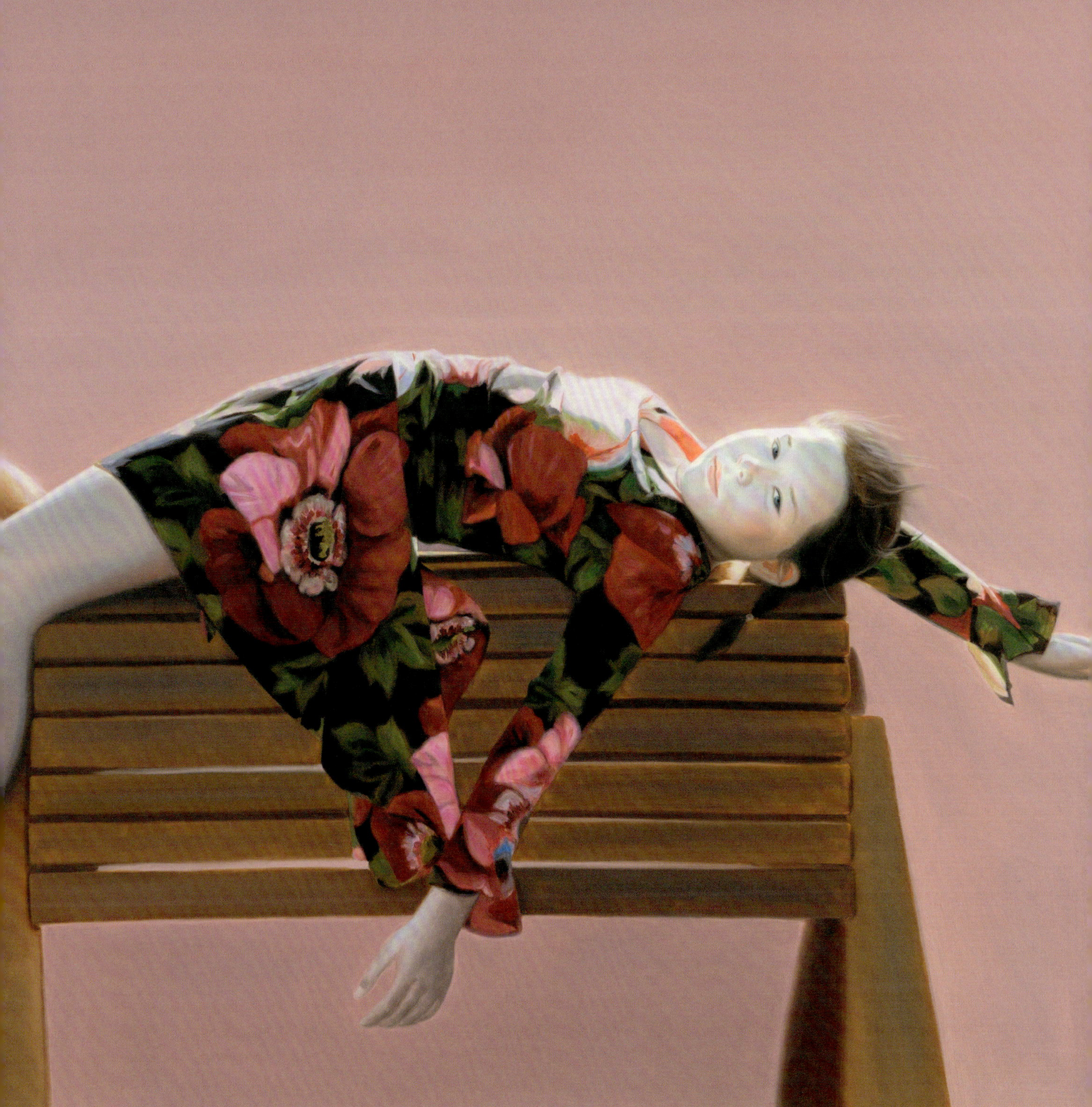

I am a Cloud 04, 2023
110 x 150 cm
Oil on canvas

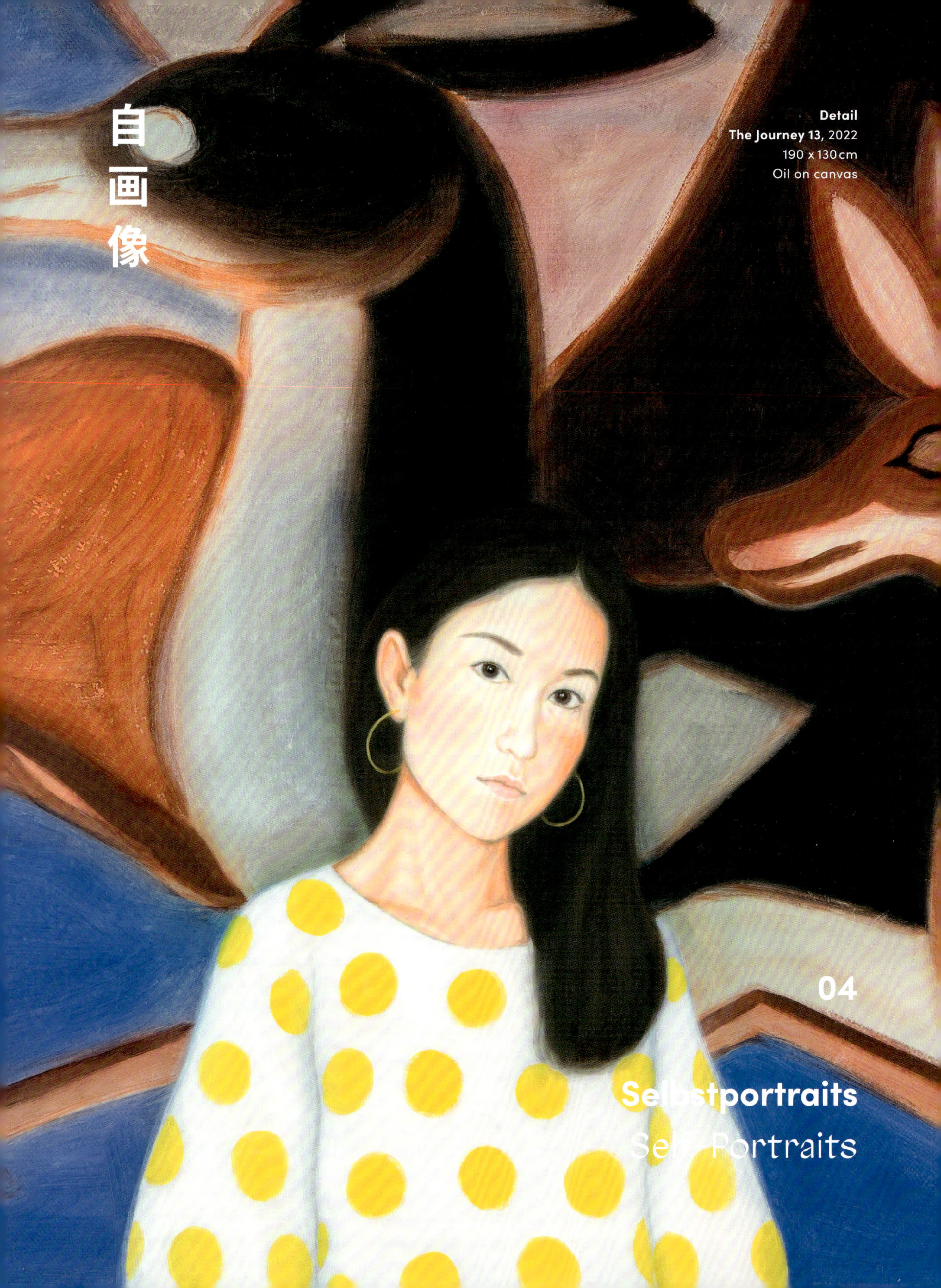

自画像

Detail
The Journey 13, 2022
190 x 130 cm
Oil on canvas

04

Selbstportraits
Self-Portraits

Haiying Xu malt regelmäßig Selbstporträts. Dieses künstlerische Motiv, das eigene Selbstverständnis ins Bild zu setzen, ist nach und nach zu einem unverzichtbaren Segment im Gesamtwerk der Künstlerin geworden. Nimmt man alle Selbstporträts der letzten 20 Jahre zusammen, so lässt sich eine deutliche Entwicklung des künstlerischen Ausdrucks von Haiying Xu feststellen. Es wäre daher eine grobe Vereinfachung zu behaupten, es ginge in ihren Selbstporträts um die Frage der Identität, auch wenn die Künstlerin dem zustimmen würde. Aber es ist eine Identität, die mit sprachlichen Mitteln nicht wiederzugeben ist, weil sie in ihrer mikrokosmischen Komplexität mobilisiert.
Diese dynamische Veränderung spürt Haiying Xu intuitiv, wenn sie sich mit der Frage der Identität auseinandersetzt. Vor diesem Hintergrund kann man ihre Selbstporträts als eine Art Inszenierung verstehen, wie sich die Künstlerin in ihren verschiedenen Lebensphasen in den jeweiligen persönlich erlebten Kontexten verortet hat.

Die handwerkliche Fähigkeit der Künstlerin, ihre Selbstbetrachtung bis ins Detail zu begleiten, hinterlässt dem Betrachter in ihrer Bildsprache präzise Beschreibungen der Gedanken, die der Künstlerin beim Blick in den Spiegel durch den Kopf gehen. Haiying Xu ist sich ihrer Selbstporträts bewusst. Das Bewusstsein ist das Reich der Illusion. Was wir vor unseren Augen sehen, sind zwar oberflächlich betrachtet einvernehmliche Selbstporträts einer Malerin. Auf einer tieferen Ebene können wir jedoch laute Gedanken der schaffenden Person rezipieren, wie diese Person sich in ihrer eigenen Gedankenwelt inszeniert. Mit vergleichbaren Inszenierungstechniken hat Frida Kahlo ihre Selbstporträts geschaffen. Auf den Ölgemälden ist zwar die Künstlerin selbst zu sehen, aber ihre Erscheinung steht immer in Relation zu ihrer Vorstellung von der eigenen Identität.

In den Selbstporträts von Haiying Xu finden wir eine Fülle von Informationen über die mentalen Bewegungen der Künstlerin. Die Informationen beschreiben, wie ihre Gedanken gedeihen. Haiying Xu stellt sich immer in ihren historischen und kulturellen Kontext, wenn sie sich selbst betrachtet. Haiying Xu ist eine Meisterin der Inszenierung. Was wir sehen, sind die Prozesse der gedanklichen Bewegung dieser denkenden, fühlenden Person, wie sie fabuliert.

Haiying Xu liebt es, sich selbst in einem Ausschnitt eines Kontextes darzustellen. Die Grundidee des Selbstporträts hat sie in der Arbeit „Ich bin in der Tür" veranschaulicht. Sie interessiert sich für Ornamente, wie sie in den Wandmalereien der Dunhuang-Grotte（敦煌莫高窟）zu finden sind. Die einheitliche Gestaltungsform durch wiederkehrende Ordnungsprinzipien der ornamentalen Elemente inspiriert die Künstlerin, deren Bewusstsein durch ihr Designstudium geprägt ist. Sie entwirft für ihr Selbstporträt eine sorgfältige Mode, die dem gewählten ornamentalen Ausschnitt entspricht. Denn Textilien stehen im Mittelpunkt von Haiying Xus malerischem Konzept. Der stoffliche Ausdruck spiegelt ihren künstlerischen Umgang mit dem Ornament wider.

Letztlich suchen wir in ihren Selbstporträts die Antwort auf die Frage: Wer ist Haiying Xu? In dem tiefen Eindruck, den wir von ihren Selbstporträts haben, sehen wir eine anmutige, entspannte Frau. Sie reagiert sensibel auf ihre Umgebung und baut eine inspirierende Beziehung zu den Welten auf, in denen sie lebt, fühlt und malt.

Haiying Xu regularly paints self-portraits. This artistic subject of depicting one's own understanding of oneself has become an indispensable part of the artist's complete works. By gathering all the self-portraits she has created over the past 20 years, a clear evolution of Haiying Xu's artistic expression is clear to see. It would be a gross oversimplification to claim that her self-portraits are simply about the question of identity, even if the artist would agree to this. But it is an identity that cannot be conveyed by means of language because it is mobilized in microcosmic complexity. Haiying Xu intuitively senses this dynamic shift when she deals with the question of identity. Against this backdrop, her self-portraits can be understood as a mise-en-scène of sorts, depicting how the artist situated herself in various contexts that she experienced herself in different phases of her life.

The artisanal ability of the artist to include such a high level of detail in her self-examination provides the onlooker with precise pictorial descriptions of the thoughts that go through the artist's mind when she looks at herself in the mirror. Haiying Xu is conscious

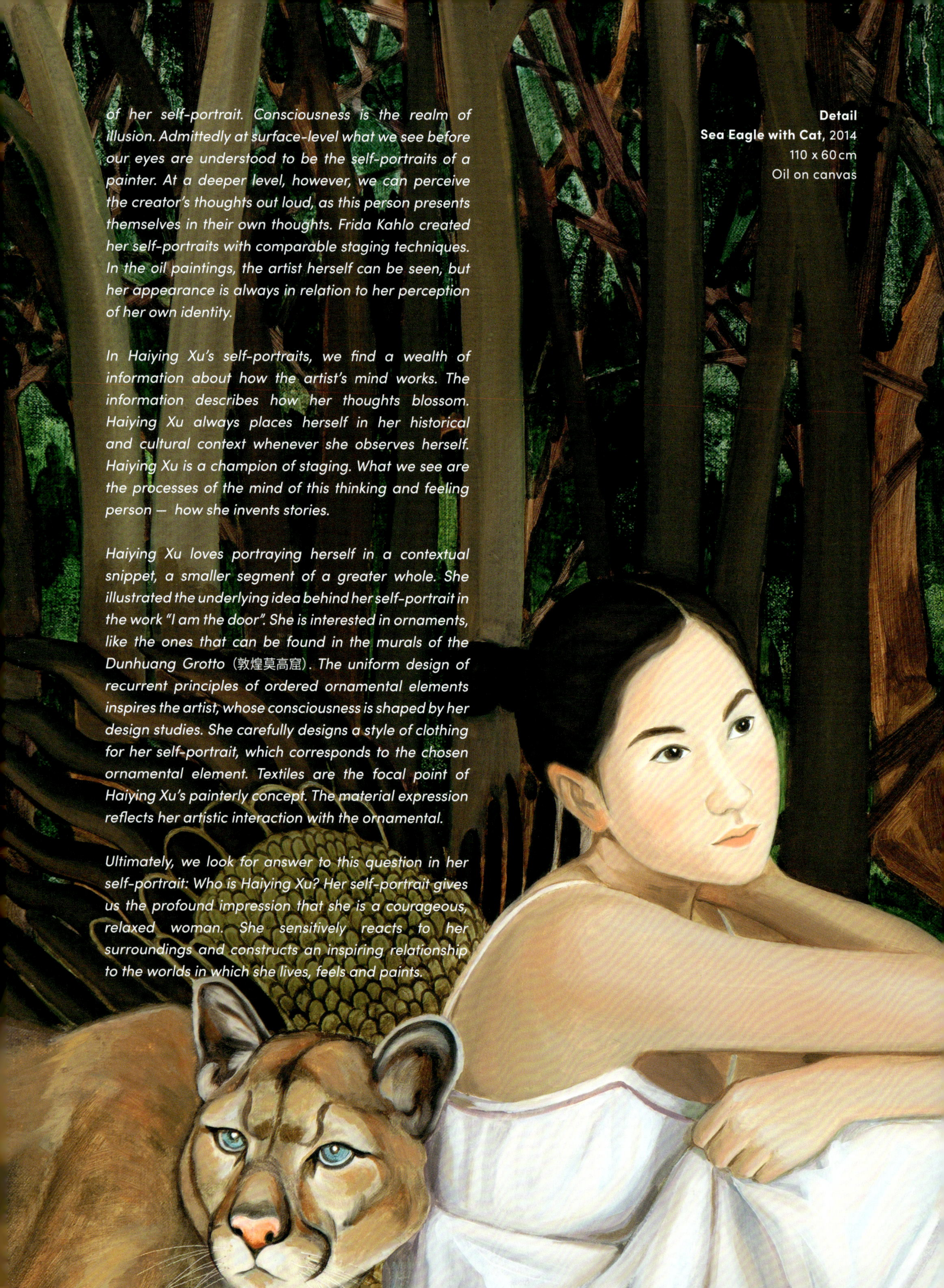

of her self-portrait. Consciousness is the realm of illusion. Admittedly at surface-level what we see before our eyes are understood to be the self-portraits of a painter. At a deeper level, however, we can perceive the creator's thoughts out loud, as this person presents themselves in their own thoughts. Frida Kahlo created her self-portraits with comparable staging techniques. In the oil paintings, the artist herself can be seen, but her appearance is always in relation to her perception of her own identity.

In Haiying Xu's self-portraits, we find a wealth of information about how the artist's mind works. The information describes how her thoughts blossom. Haiying Xu always places herself in her historical and cultural context whenever she observes herself. Haiying Xu is a champion of staging. What we see are the processes of the mind of this thinking and feeling person — how she invents stories.

Haiying Xu loves portraying herself in a contextual snippet, a smaller segment of a greater whole. She illustrated the underlying idea behind her self-portrait in the work "I am the door". She is interested in ornaments, like the ones that can be found in the murals of the Dunhuang Grotto（敦煌莫高窟）. The uniform design of recurrent principles of ordered ornamental elements inspires the artist, whose consciousness is shaped by her design studies. She carefully designs a style of clothing for her self-portrait, which corresponds to the chosen ornamental element. Textiles are the focal point of Haiying Xu's painterly concept. The material expression reflects her artistic interaction with the ornamental.

Ultimately, we look for answer to this question in her self-portrait: Who is Haiying Xu? Her self-portrait gives us the profound impression that she is a courageous, relaxed woman. She sensitively reacts to her surroundings and constructs an inspiring relationship to the worlds in which she lives, feels and paints.

Detail
Sea Eagle with Cat, 2014
110 x 60 cm
Oil on canvas

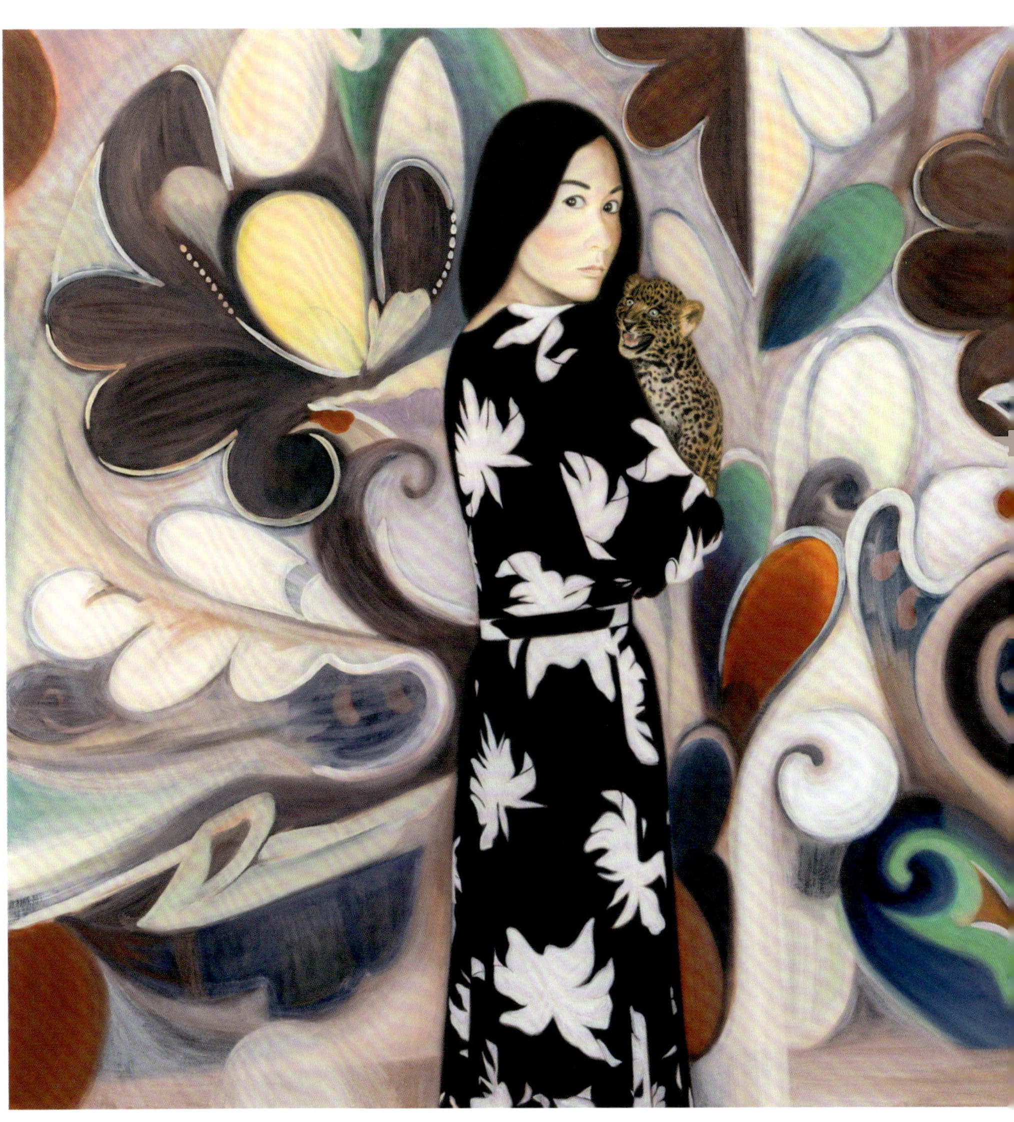

December 2020, 2021
110 x 110 cm
Oil on canvas

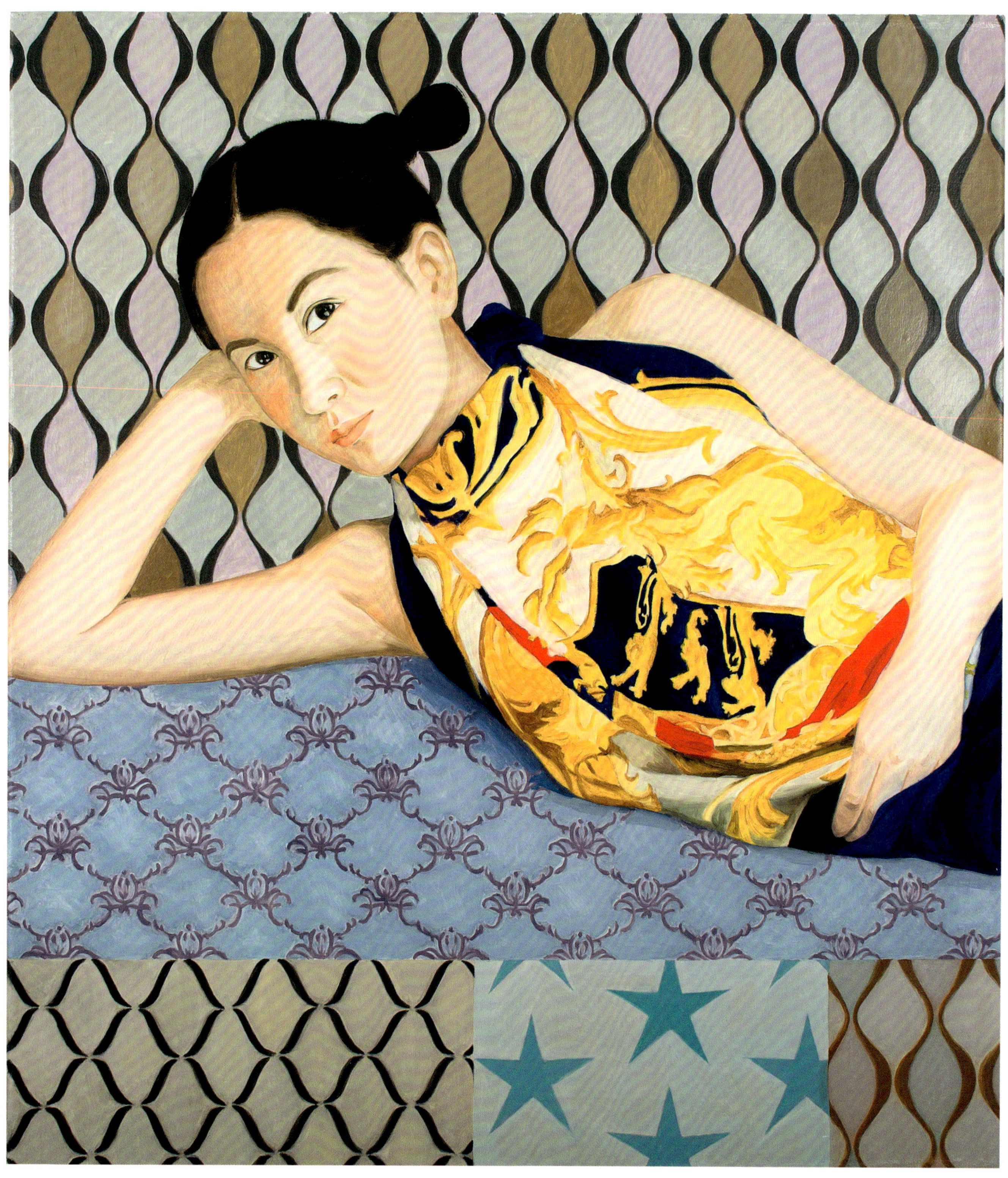

Self-Portrait 10, 2012
90 x 80 cm
Oil on canvas

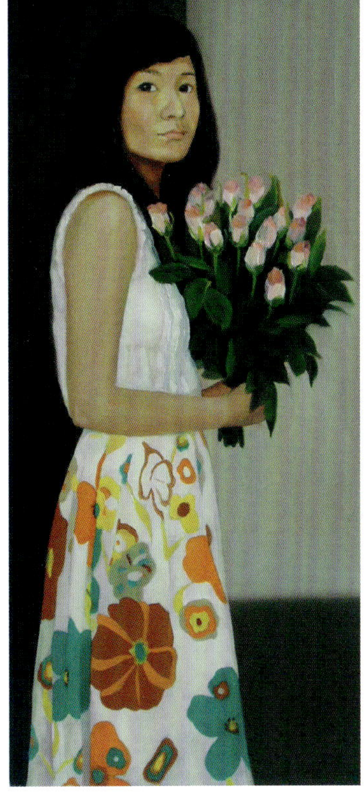

Me in the door 02, 2006
190 x 210 cm
Oil on canvas

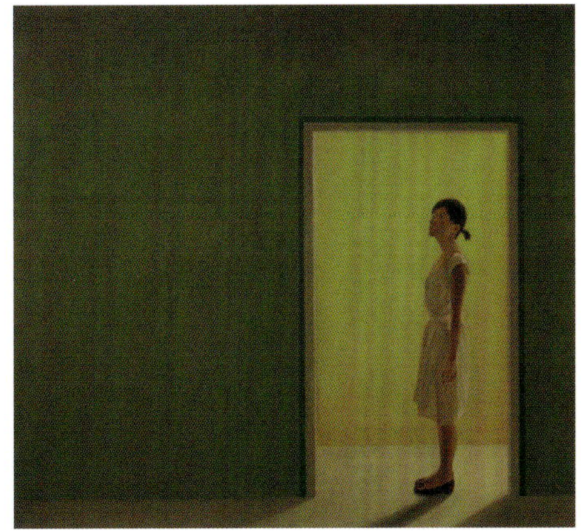

Self-Portrait 04, 2004
110 x 50 cm
Oil on canvas

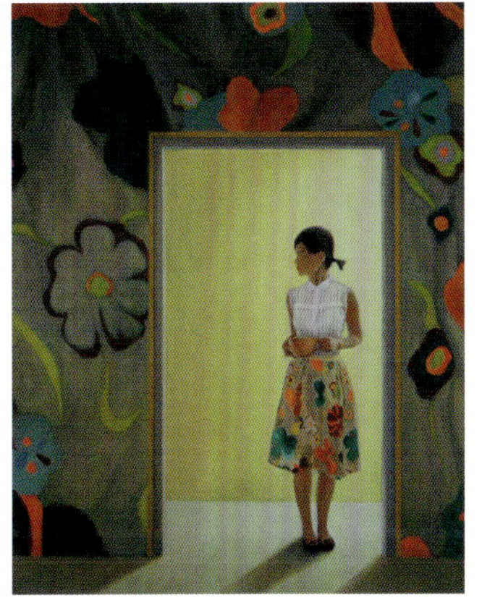

Me in the door 01, 2006
190 x 150 cm
Oil on canvas

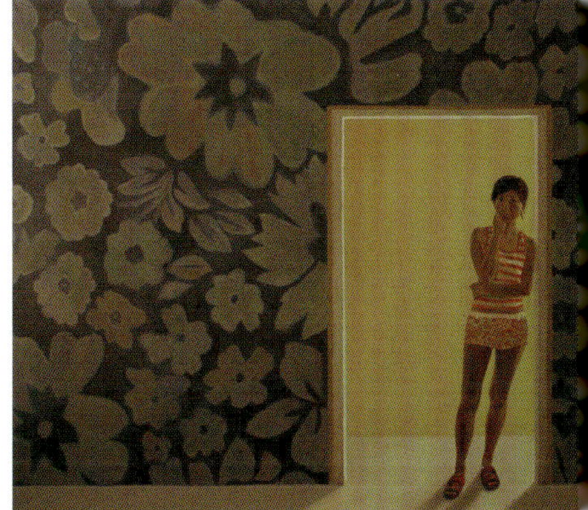

Me in the door 03, 2006
190 x 230 cm
Oil on canvas

Me and Ornament 04, 2006
140 x 190 cm
Oil on canvas

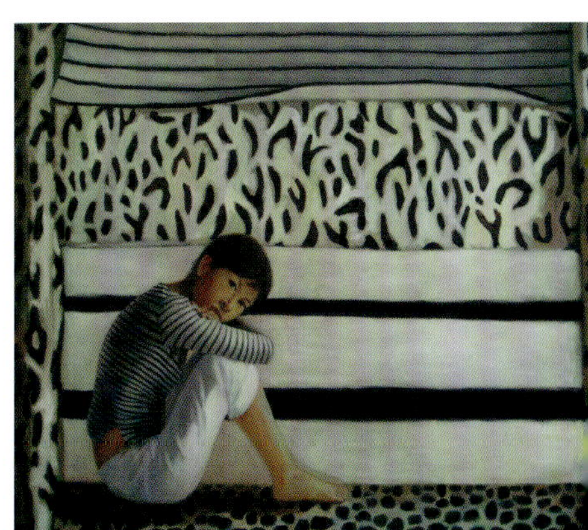

徐海鹰

Sea Eagle 09, 2011
80 x 90 cm
Oil on canvas

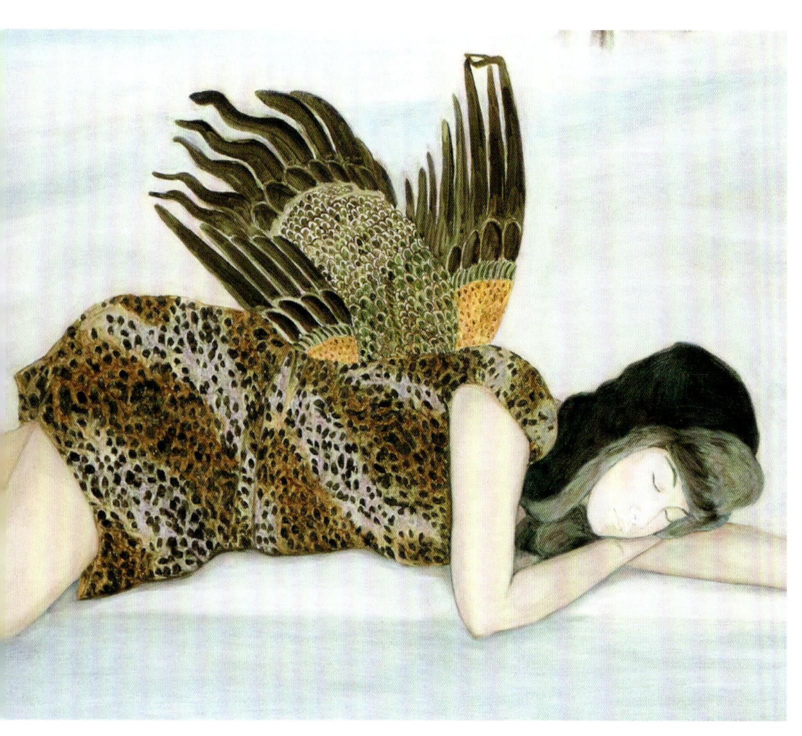

Haiying Xu
Biography

1975 geboren in Jiangxi, China

1993-1996 Design-Studium an der Hainan University, China

2003-2009 Studium der Malerei bei Professorin Anke Doberauer, Akademie der Bildenden Künste, München

2009 Diplom und DAAD-Auszeichnung für ausländische Studierende

2009 Meisterschülerin bei Professorin Anke Doberauer

2016 Reise nach Südchina, u.a. Sanbaishan

Sie lebt und arbeitet in München

Einzelausstellungen

2024 Dreihundert Berge, Galerie Andreas Binder, München (Katalog)

2019 Ferne Welten, weiter Träumen, St. Annen Museum, Lübeck (Katalog)

2018 Sanbaishan, Galerie Andreas Binder, München

2015 Du und Sie und Wir, Galerie Andreas Binder, München

2010 Seeadler, Galerie Andreas Binder, München (Katalog)

Gruppenausstellungen

2023 Haubentaucher I, Alte Handelsschule, Leipzig
Haubentaucher II, Galerie Weise, Chemnitz
Haubentaucher III, Galerie im Malzhaus, Plauen
Haubentaucher IV, Halle 50 Domagkateliers, München

2022 Das kleine Format, Blaues Haus, Ammersee

2021 The show must go on, Galerie Andreas Binder, München
FOR FREE* - artists are not working for free. Eine Intervention von Daniel Man in der Galerie Andreas Binder, München

2020 Traumtänzer. Gemälde und Bronzen von Hanne Kroll und Haiying Xu, Galerie Weise, Chemnitz

2019 Freischein, Galerie Weise, Chemnitz

2018 Eden Now, Galerie Andreas Binder, München

2017 Wir, Galerie Weise, Chemnitz

2015 Skill-Base-Painting, art bv Berchtoldvilla, Salzburg

2014 Menschen, Tiere und Kanonen. Vom Leben der Vereine, Kunsthalle Rostock (Katalog)

2013 Macht Heimat!, Draiflessen Collection, Mettingen (Katalog)

2012 Peeneaale 2012, Kunstverein Loitz

2010 Biennale „mulhouse 010“, Frankreich (Katalog)

2009 Debütantenausstellung 2009, Akademie der Bildenden Künste, München
Diplomausstellung, Akademie der Bildenden Künste, München

2008 Jubiläumsausstellung, Kunstverein Ebersberg e.V. Galerie "Alte Brennerei", Ebersberg
Augen-Blick 2.0 – Mirroring China, Berlin UdK

2007 Mahlverwandtschaften II, Goethe-Institute, München

2006 Lineup, Drawings, Kulturverein Modern Studio Freising e.V., Freising
Gallery of the Academy of Art, Budapest, Ungarn
Sun every Day, Galerie Art Ambassador, München

2005 Klassenprojekt "Mauerwerke", Ausstellung bei der Bundesgartenschau München

Preise

2022 Katalogförderung Erwin und Gisela von Steiner Stiftung

2019 Stipendium aus dem „Programm zur Realisierung der Chancengleichheit für Frauen in Forschung und Lehre“ von der Akademie der Bildenden Künste München

2011 Stipendium Loitzer Kunstverein e.V.

2010 Prix du Conseil Général du Haut-Rhin
Katalogförderung Erwin und Gisela von Steiner Stiftung
Katalogförderung LFA Förderbank Bayern

2009 Diplom mit Auszeichnung – DAAD Preis für hervorragende Leistungen ausländischer Studierenden

2008 Junge Kunst in Bayern, Kunstkalender 2009 der LFA Förderbank Bayern

1975 born in Jiangxi, China

1993-1996 Design studies at Hainan University, China

2003-2009 studied painting under Professor Anke Doberauer at the Academy of Fine Arts, Munich

2009 Diploma and DAAD award for foreign students

2009 Master student under Professor Anke Doberauer

2016 Journey to Southchina, a.o. Sanbaishan

Lives and works in Munich

Solo Exhibitions

2024 Dreihundert Berge, Galerie Andreas Binder, Munich (catalogue)

2019 Ferne Welten, weiter Träumen, St. Annen Museum, Luebeck, Germany (catalogue)

2018 Sanbaishan, Galerie Andreas Binder, Munich

2015 Du und Sie und Wir, Galerie Andreas Binder, Munich

2010 Seeadler, Galerie Andreas Binder, Munich (catalogue)

Group Exhibitions

2023 Haubentaucher I, Alte Handelsschule, Leipzig, Germany
Haubentaucher II, Galerie Weise, Chemnitz, Germany
Haubentaucher III, Galerie in the Malzhaus, Plauen, Germany
Haubentaucher IV, Halle 50 Domagkateliers, Munich

2022 Das kleine Format, Blaues Haus, Ammersee, Germany

2021 The show must go on, Galerie Andreas Binder, Munich
FOR FREE* - artists are not working for free. An intervention by Daniel Man at Galerie Andreas Binder, Munich

2020 Traumtänzer. Gemälde und Bronzen von Hanne Kroll und Haiying Xu, Galerie Weise, Chemnitz, Germany

2019 Freischein, Galerie Weise, Chemnitz, Germany

2018 Eden now, Galerie Andreas Binder, Munich

2017 Wir, Galerie Weise, Chemnitz, Germany

2015 Skill-Base-Painting, art bv, Berchtoldvilla, Salzburg, Austria

2014 Menschen, Tiere und Kanonen. Vom Leben der Vereine, Kunsthalle Rostock, Germany (catalogue)

2013 Macht Heimat!, Draiflessen Mettingen, Germany (catalogue)

2012 Peeneaale 2012, Kunstverein Loitz, Germany

2010 Biennale "mulhouse 010", France (catalogue)

2009 Debutant exhibition 2009, Academy of Fine Arts, Munich
Diploma exhibition, Academy of Fine Arts, Munich

2008 Annual exhibition Kunstverein Ebersberg e.V. Galerie "Alte Brennerei", Ebersberg, Germany
Augen-Blick 2.0 – Mirroring China, Berlin UdK, Germany

2007 Mahlverwandtschaften II, Goethe-Institute, Munich

2006 Lineup, Drawings, Kulturverein Modern Studio Freising e.V., Freising, Germany
Gallery of the Academy of Art, Budapest, Hungary
Sun every Day, Galerie Art Ambassador, Munich

2005 Mauerwerke, Exhibition at Bundesgartenschau, Munich

Awards

2022 Catalogue Funding by Erwin and Gisela von Steiner Foundation

2019 Scholarship from the "Program for the realization of equal opportunities for women in research and teaching" from the Academy of Fine Arts Munich

2011 Scholarship Loitzer Kunstverein e.V.

2010 Prix du Conseil Général du Haut-Rhin
Catalogue Funding by Erwin and Gisela von Steiner Foundation
Catalogue Funding by LFA Förderbank Bayern

2009 Diploma with distinction - DAAD prize for outstanding achievements of foreign students

2008 Young art in Bavaria, art calendar 2009 of the LFA Förderbank Bayern